"Fantastic, inspiri dissects life as a yo Christ in a modern world. I hope to follow his advice and guidance as I continue my journey and walk with Christ. As a newcomer to the world of adulting, I'm thankful for Bruce and everything he does to help my generation succeed both materially and spiritually. I hope this book blesses you as much as it did for me."

—Frannie Haller, High School Math Teacher

"Bruce pours out his soul as he shares the pain and challenges of growing up in an abusive family, which led to years of self-abuse as a young adult. In his current book, *A Well-Launched Life*, Bruce details how it took God coming into his life to save him from his destructive ways and put him on a path with real purpose and meaning. Through his years of experience in corporate America and as a Christian father who raised four young adults, Bruce provides practical ways to help young adults plan and take control of their lives. A must-read for anyone struggling to figure out how to actually plan for a successful and fulfilling life and why it needs to include God at its center."

—Tad Orr, Business Communications Manager, Major US Bank

"One of life's greatest beauties is when our raw and often debilitating experiences are transformed into priceless diamonds, which launch us and others into a hopeful future. That is what Bruce masterfully does in his book, *A Well-Launched Life*. The book is applicable to people in all stages of life, and it's especially transformational for young adults between the ages of eighteen and twenty-eight years. Bruce's wealth of wisdom has the potential to launch you to heights in your prime that many can't reach in a lifetime."

—Lianna Doty, Relationship Manager/ Women's Director at Urban KLife

"The answer to question eleven in the Westminster Shorter Catechism describes God's providence. My son and I had been given a copy of *Traction* by a client and quickly determined that we needed to look for a Certified EOS Implementer to help us incorporate these techniques into our business and corporate culture.

After placing calls and talking to a couple of implementers, my son noticed the email signature of an acquaintance from church with whom he was working on a Bible study. The signature included the title Certified EOS Implementer, the acquaintance was Bruce Sheridan, and once again we were the benefactors of God's wise, governing providence.

Today I am blessed to call Bruce my friend and when he described this book project, I encouraged him to do for another generation what he had done for us. Life Compass is much more than what he did for us. I am convinced that Life Compass has a much higher call than to help a business find their way and culture post acquisition, I expect to hear for years to come the testimonies of lives having found purpose and direction by owning these concepts. There is no higher goal than discipling another in the ways of God."

— Bradley Greer, President, EIA Consulting

"What an extraordinary symphony of truth and instruction. From Bruce's harsh experiences in the early stages of his life and discovering God's hand through it all, to gaining training and wisdom to create a presentation of very practical,

God-centered ways to develop successful, sure-footed paths regardless of one's field of choice or goals to be attained."

—Deborah Hendrickson, Manager, Business Leader, Mentor

"Bruce Sheridan's exposure to a vast array of life experiences gives him a unique platform of insight and relatability into the hearts of our youth, and his vulnerability and humility provide a sense of trust. Thank you, Bruce, for your investment in the lives of young adults by giving them a framework for success to grab hold of in a world of inconsistencies and extreme chatter. The Biblical principles shared intertwined with achievable, actionable steps will provide resilience through the life challenges they will encounter. Why fly blind when there's a roadmap for achieving a life well-lived within these pages?"

—Brooke Graham, Managing Partner, duvari

"I am convinced that a *A Well-Launched Life* will provide powerful strategies and proven concepts that will help young adults plan and live a God-centered life. God has equipped Bruce with intellectual capital that can help young adults live an intentional life. Our young adults should not be the victims of a purpose-less life. Bruce Sheridan is a qualified and well-respected professional facilitator/instructor/coach who specializes in developing leaders, corporate executives, and people who possess a heart to achieve."

—Julius Sims, Ed.D., Managing Director of Urban KLife

"Bruce and I met in a men's Bible Study and became instant friends because we both love God and both played defensive ends in high school football. Bruce hadn't told me about his rough start in life. I couldn't stop reading his life story once I started it. It is truly a witness to the love of God, and the strength of God to draw a person close to Himself—ultimately sheltering Bruce under His wings."

—***Bill Lapp, Defensive End***

"Bruce artfully communicates to young adults why this time in their lives is so critical by humbly sharing examples of the harmful decisions he made during those years. He has a passion for helping others avoid the mistakes he made with specific advice and by helping them set a course for a lifetime of success rooted in their unique God-given purpose. I only wish he would have written this book thirty-five years ago, so I could have avoided some of the snares of the world. I fully intend to share this brilliant book with all the young people God entrusts me to disciple."

—***Greg Hoffmann, Owner, Ryze Adventure Park***

"Bruce's story is incredible, and he's an open book. He shares a litany of poor decisions he made as a young man in hopes of equipping others—male and female—that there's a better way to live. As I've gotten to know Bruce, I've been encouraged to understand the tools that he's created to help young men and women live lives of purpose. Lives are fulfilled when they're launched well."

—***Greg Atchison, Principal Chair,***
C12 Greater Saint Louis

A WELL-LAUNCHED LIFE

ROGER

TO MY BROTHER IN CHRIST!

Roger

To my brother in Christ!

A WELL-LAUNCHED LIFE

How Young People Can Live an Intentional, Fulfilling Life

BRUCE SHERIDAN

Stonebrook Publishing
Saint Louis, Missouri

A STONEBROOK PUBLISHING BOOK

This book was guided in development
by Nancy L. Erickson, The Book Professor®
TheBookProfessor.com

Library of Congress Control Number: 2021918832

Paperback ISBN: 978-1-955711-07-4
eBook ISBN: 978-1-955711-08-1

www.stonebrookpublishing.net
PRINTED IN THE UNITED STATES OF AMERICA

This book is dedicated to God. To my wife Jan.
To our four sons; Andrew and his wife Monica
and their daughter Luna, Nicholas, Mark, and Charlie.
God has blessed me with my family. I love them dearly.

CONTENTS

1

HARD BEGINNINGS

For you created my inmost being; you knit me together in my mother's womb. I praise you because I am fearfully and wonderfully made; your works are wonderful, I know that full well. My frame was not hidden from you when I was made in the secret place, when I was woven together in the depths of the earth. Your eyes saw my unformed body; . . .

Psalm 139:13-1

For many of us, the safest place we've ever been is in our mother's womb. I was knit together in my mother's womb in Union City, New Jersey, between 1958 and 1959. My earliest memory is when I was a toddler, just two-and-a-half. My mom and dad had gone out for the evening, and they left my three older siblings and me with my father's sister, Aunt Joan. When they returned home, they found me in a bad state. I was sick. My mom pulled out the humidifier, filled it with water, globbed a few fingerfuls of Vicks VapoRub into a small well where the steam came out. She plugged it in and set it on the end table next to her bed. My crib, however, was past the foot of her bed, shoved into the corner of the room. As my mom lay down to fall asleep, I kept her awake with my coughing and wheezing. Her maternal instincts took over, and she got up, lifted me out of the crib, and took me into her bed, so I could be closer to the humidifier. She snuggled me close, and we fell asleep.

I'm not exactly sure when it happened, but sometime that night, I rolled out of the bed. I landed on the humidifier cord and yanked it off the end table, breaking its glass body and spilling the boiling water and liquified Vicks VapoRub all over me. I screamed at the top of my lungs.

My father jumped out of bed and picked me up, burning his feet. A fireman, Dad knew to grab a clean white sheet out of the dresser drawer and wrap me in it. He raced me to the bathtub and turned on the cold water. He knew the temperature of my skin needed to be cooled, or it would continue to cook. He plunged me into the cold water. Mom watched over me as Dad called the hospital to alert them that he was on his way with a burn victim. Dad grabbed me, raced out of the house, put me in the back seat of his car, and sped to the hospital. I looked up through the big rear window at the night sky.

Christ Hospital is a towering facility that sits atop the Palisades in Jersey City, New Jersey. It opened its doors in 1872; today, it has 376 beds. If you enter New Jersey from Manhattan through the Holland Tunnel, you can see Christ Hospital on top of several hundred feet of rock, not only because it's a campus of large buildings but also because large letters spell out "Christ Hospital" on the top of the building. Even at night from across the Hudson River in Manhattan, you can see the name lit up in large white letters.

My dad pulled up, got me out of the back seat, and carried me to a team of doctors and nurses as they hurried out to meet us. They rushed me into the building and through halls and corridors into a tucked-away room. In that room, the staff had prepared a large bathtub half filled with water and half filled with ice. The doctor dunked me into the tub and tried to roll me around lengthwise in the icy mixture to completely stop the burning process. I fought him with all my strength because I thought he was trying to dunk my head under the water. I could tell he couldn't believe how strong I was.

Finally, he got a good hold on me, covered my nose and mouth with his hand, and rolled me over. When my head went under the icy water, I blacked out.

The doctors told my parents I wouldn't live through the night. I had severe third-degree burns on my left leg, left arm, and the left side of my back, and I was fighting a sinus and lung infection. But God had different plans for me, and I made it through the night and many nights after.

I stayed in the hospital for six weeks, living in a large crib in a large room with many other cribs. The nurses were kind to me, and Mom came to visit me every day. When she left, I would cry and cry and cry. Three times a day, the nurses gave me a shot of penicillin in my buttocks. Of course, I fought them every time. I knew when they were coming because it took three of them to hold me down and one to inject me. When the four nurses started walking toward me, I'd start to cry and scream. Three shots a day for six weeks, seven days a week—126 shots! When I finally went home, my bottom had red dots in various stages of healing on both sides.

The worst part was when Dr. Prince, my pediatrician, came to see me. I never knew if it was going to be a bad visit until he picked me up out of my crib. That meant he was going to take me to the bathtub. He'd sit me on the edge of the tub and lay out a white cloth beside me. My back was so severely burned that pieces of my burned skin hung from my body. Dr. Prince would take a pair of pliers, grab the hanging skin, and tear it off my body, laying the strips of skin on the cloth next to me. He continued until I shook from head to toe, overcome with pain.

Later, when I was older, Dr. Prince explained that they had to pull off the dead skin to keep an infection from developing in the crevice where the skin met my body. Even worse, the skin hanging off my back could get caught on something and be ripped off my body, which would cause extreme pain and might require stitches. Pulling off the dead skin allowed new skin to grow.

After six months, I had healed, but to this day, I live with the scars from the burn. It was always difficult for me to go to a swimming pool or to the beach. When I was wearing a bathing suit, over 90 percent of my scar was exposed, and I felt insecure. Strangers—mostly children—would ask me what happened, and I'd tell them how I got burned. I remember so many details of that ordeal, yet I don't remember anything else from my early childhood until I went to kindergarten.

Elementary School

My parents were parishioners at the Saint Anthony's Catholic Church in Union City, New Jersey. Union City is the proud home of the entrance to the Lincoln Tunnel that connects New Jersey to Midtown Manhattan, New York City. It's renowned for being the second-most densely populated city in the

United States. Union City is 1.1 square miles with over 60,000 residents. The New Jersey side of the Hudson River sits on top of a palisade. Living on top of a palisade made for fantastic views of the Manhattan skyline at night.

St. Anthony's was a large church, which also housed an elementary school. The buildings were made of light-colored tan bricks, and it took up an entire block. My family attended services regularly. Mom and Dad were on committees, my older brothers were altar boys, and we were encouraged to go to confession every week.

I attended St. Anthony's School from kindergarten through third grade. I was a good student, but I got into trouble all the time. The nuns smacked my hands and bottom with rulers and yardsticks. The Sister Superior sent notes home to my parents, and on the way home, I threw the notes down the sewer. Big mistake.

When my parents came in for parent/teacher night, Sister Superior cornered them and asked why they'd never answered her notes. Both of my parents were embarrassed. They made a deal that Sister Superior would give any notes to my older brother to bring home. Whenever he got a note, he tormented me all the way home. I'd try to take the note from him, but he was too strong and much bigger than me.

I knew what would happen when my dad read the note. It would ignite his sense of discipline—and he would beat me. A lot depended on his mood. The beating could be severe or mild. I never knew what to expect.

My parents had two more children, which put a serious strain on our family's finances. No longer able to afford private school, my parents sent me to the public school. There, things got interesting. Even though I'd lived in the same neighborhood since I was born, I was the new kid in school. That meant the bullies wanted to fight me. After school, I had to carefully navigate my way home to avoid the wrong classmates. Every so often, I was cornered. I learned it was better to fight and lose than to simply lose. The bullies would rather beat up a kid who didn't hit back versus one who did. So I chose to hit back.

I was the fourth child born into our family, and before I was born, my family lived in low-income housing. Single-story, brick row houses with adjoining walls ran on for ten housing units. The front yards were small dirt patches with clotheslines. On Saturdays, almost every front yard had laundry on the lines. People called this area the "Projects." If you lived in the Projects, you were poor.

When I was born, my parents decided we needed more room, but my dad couldn't afford a single-family home. So he bought a three-family house and rented out the other two apartments to help pay for the house. When they added two more children to our brood, we were once again bursting at the seams.

We moved six blocks up and two avenues over. Moving a few blocks doesn't sound like much, but in my microcosm of a world, it might as well have been another planet. They bought a big, old house that had previously been a hospital. It had four oversized marble fireplaces, two on the first floor and two on the second floor. You could tell by the layout that there had been a waiting room, an exam room, and a surgery room.

That year would change my life. A new neighborhood meant a new school, and there were four terrors in my fourth-grade class. The teacher had no control over the classroom. The gang of four would lash out at any classmate at any moment. One day, one of them, whom I'll call Tom, brought a large diaper pin to school. He bent it apart so that it formed a three-inch steel pin. When I was leaning over a desk talking to Cindy Hawkins, a girl I had a crush on, Tom came up behind me, wound up his arm like a windmill, and slammed that diaper pin into my buttocks. The tip of the pin hit a bone, which stopped it from going further in. I was so shocked; I didn't know what had hit me.

A few days later, there was a black-and-blue bruise on my bottom as big around as a tennis ball. After that, my mom marched me into the principal's office and made me drop my pants. The principal was so horrified, he marched up to our classroom and made me point out Tom. He grabbed Tom out of his seat, dragged him to the front of the class, picked him up under his arms, and slammed his back into the wall about eight feet up. Tom didn't bother me for about two days after that episode.

That year, the gang of four broke our teacher's foot. She'd taken one of them out into the hall to reprimand him, and he stomped on her foot as hard as he could. She wore a cast and was on crutches for six weeks. Another one-on-one hall reprimand resulted in her broken finger. As she waved her index finger in his face and scolded him, the boy reached up to grab her finger, caught her pinky, and tried to rip it off. That, too, was in a cast for six weeks. In another hall reprimand, one of the gang reached up and tore her glasses off her face. Holding both arms of the frame, he pulled them apart, and the glasses snapped in two. She taped them together with a big wad of white tape until she could get new ones, which took weeks. She looked like a crazy lady with black cat-eye glasses taped together at the bridge of her nose.

About twice a month, the gang would say out loud, "We are not learning right now." Then they'd walk up to the teacher, take her book off her desk, and throw it across the room. The four of them would then walk around the room and push everyone's books off their desks. One day the teacher tried to resist, and the gang pushed her steel desk over on top of her.

Every day was complete chaos. Our classroom had a small rectangular fish tank, probably twenty to thirty gallons. The gang pushed it over on its stand, and it crashed down onto the hardwood floor. The glass walls of the tank exploded, and the fish and water went everywhere.

The following year, two of the gang went to fifth grade at a school for troubled students. Fifth grade was pretty good without those two, and the teacher, Mrs. Buhlman, was tough. Whenever I'm asked the security question, "Who was your favorite teacher?" I answer Buhlman. She restored normalcy in our classroom.

Some days when I walked home from school, when I got to the corner, I could hear my father yelling in our house. Since our neighbors' houses were just a few feet away, they would occasionally ask my mom if everything was all right because they heard him shouting several times a week. There was a metal street sign on that corner that identified West Street and 16th Street. If I reached that pole and could hear my dad's raised voice, I wouldn't go home. Sometimes it could take up to fifteen to twenty minutes for him to stop. After he stopped, I waited at least five more minutes to make sure he was done. If one of us walked into the house when he was screaming, we'd get a hard smack to the back of the head, at a minimum.

One day an elderly woman walked by. She stopped and asked, "Young man, what are you doing standing here on the corner? Are you okay? Where do you live?"

I was embarrassed and afraid to tell her, but I mustered up my courage and said, "I can hear my dad yelling, and I don't want to go home until he stops."

I could tell she was stunned and didn't know what to say. After she thought about it, she asked, "Are you sure you're okay?"

"Yes, I'll be fine," I said.

She walked away. I could tell she was upset but didn't know what to do. In the 1960s, people didn't call the police about domestic abuse. She walked away, shaking her head in disbelief.

The abuse was generational. My grandfather had physically and verbally abused my father, and my father carried on the twisted habit. I wasn't the only target; my five siblings and my mom were not spared. Something would set my dad off, and if you were in range, he'd smack you in the back of the head or kick you in the butt with his size thirteen shoe. Sometimes when he was upset, I'd get a beating. If he didn't give me a punishment chore, I went to my room and stayed there for hours.

I shared a room with my two older brothers. To optimize the space, my twin bed was actually a trundle bed that folded down to the floor and rolled under my brother's bed. At night, I rolled it out, lifted it, and locked it in place. In the morning, I released the lock, folded it down, and rolled it away. The downside was that if my brother needed to get out of bed, he had to crawl over me. Most of the time, he crushed me with his elbows and knees.

When I was six or seven years old, my dad beat those brothers with a miniature souvenir baseball bat that was about fifteen inches long. And I was the cause.

I kept what little money I had in an old eyeglass case, and I had maybe $1.50. One day the money was missing.

Dad overheard me grumbling, and he asked, "What are you grumbling about?" I told him.

He called my two older brothers and made them stand in front of him in the kitchen. He asked one of them, "Did you take the money?'

"No," he said.

He wound up the mini bat and hit him so hard in the buttocks and hamstring areas that you could see the pain shoot through his body.

Then he turned to my other brother and asked, "Did you take the money?"

"No."

He received the same painful beating.

I stood there and watched this for what seemed like an eternity. Dad went back and forth between my brothers at least five times. Neither one ever admitted to taking the money. They went back to our room and cried for hours, lying on their stomachs because they couldn't turn over on their backs because of the painful beating.

Because our house had once been a hospital, the ceilings were ten to twelve feet tall, and the kitchen was a big room. It had built-in cabinets from the floor to the ceiling. The bottom third was solid wood cabinets with drawers and a counter. The top two-thirds were wooden shelves with glass doors. We kept things we rarely used on the higher shelves; we had to get out the three-step ladder to reach them. We had a large, white porcelain sink, a radiator, a large table, and a large stove. There was also a door that led to a pantry and another door from the pantry that went outside.

When I was about twelve, I was standing by the door that led to the pantry, minding my own business. My dad was pitching a fit. He walked by me and stopped. I felt sick to my stomach; I knew something was coming. Like a drill sergeant, he screamed a question in my face. I guess I gave the wrong answer because he punched me in the mouth so hard that my head bounced off the door behind me. I felt something foreign in my mouth and spit it into my hand. Dad had punched out my front tooth.

Once again, I was put in the back seat with an injury. This time we were headed to the dentist. His office was about five miles away, but it took thirty minutes to get there through the densely populated city, with many traffic lights and stop signs. On the way to his office, I told Mom I was fed up and was going to tell the dentist what happened. My mom flipped out. She began steering with her left hand while she screamed at me and leaned back over the front seat to hit me with her right hand. The car swerved all over the road. Parked cars lined the streets on both sides of the road. She was lucky not to sideswipe one of them.

"Tell the dentist you fell off your bike!" she screamed.

Because I'd received penicillin for months when I was burned as a toddler, my teeth were always in need of work. I'd visited the dentist many times, felt the pain of many needles in my gums, and I'd had my teeth drilled so often that I developed a true phobia about going to the dentist. He finally said I couldn't come back until my pediatrician prescribed tranquilizers for me to take before visits. Since this was an emergency, I didn't have time to take a tranquilizer. I sat in the waiting area, freaking out.

Finally, I was called back to the dental chair. Dr. Jerome loomed over me and asked me to explain again and again exactly how I'd knocked out my tooth on my bicycle. The bright dental light shined in my eyes and face. I began to sweat, and my nerves frayed. I wanted so badly to tell him the truth.

With a puzzled look, he kept asking, "Tell me again how you broke your tooth on your bicycle."

I could tell he wanted to know the truth as badly as I wanted to tell it. But I just couldn't. He finally gave up the question and fixed my tooth.

The worst was when Dad hit Mom. It would rock me to my core to see him hit her and berate her in front of me. Mom was always shocked when it happened and would start crying. I hated him when he hit my mom.

Finally, Dad tried to get help. He saw several psychiatrists. Around that time—I think I was twelve—our family was invited to family counseling at Mount Sinai Hospital in New York City. My mom, dad, and all six kids piled into the station wagon. We drove through the Lincoln Tunnel to Manhattan to meet the psychiatrist, a gentle, sweet woman. She assured us that whatever we said was okay and that my dad had agreed to listen. For an entire hour, we unloaded on my dad—every one of us. He sat there and listened. I think he was embarrassed, but we all felt relieved that there was a safe place where we could talk to someone about how Dad abused us.

The next week was hell. Dad was angry and took revenge. He was physically and verbally abusive at an even higher level than before. When it was time for the next therapy session, we all piled into the station wagon. No one spoke during the entire ride. In the therapy room, no one spoke.

The doctor was perplexed. She asked my dad what had happened. He looked like a five-year-old who'd just gotten into trouble; I'd never seen him like this in my life. It began to dawn on me how mentally ill he was. We made little progress that day. The following week, we spoke about how our home wasn't a safe place. The doctor did her best to help us.

A few weeks later, we were driving home, and something on the bottom of the car started to drag on the surface of the road, making a terrible noise. The kids always fought over who got to ride shotgun in the front seat. Often, my mom would sit in the second row of seats, so someone could ride next to Dad in the front. He got out and reached under the car to try to get whatever had been dragging to go back in place. He burned his hand when he grabbed the hot pipe.

He jumped up and yelled at my mom, "See what you made me do! You made me burn my hand!"

He got back in the driver's seat, twisted around to face my mom in the back seat, and told her to get out and fix it.

She said, "I'm not getting out and fixing it." It was a good thing she was in the back seat. I could tell Dad wanted to slap her.

Dad twisted around again and screamed at her, "Get out of the car and fix the damn muffler!"

Instead, she got out of the car and walked down the street. She kept walking. I could see that my dad was torn. He had a broken-down car on a New York City street with six kids in it, and his wife was briskly walking away down the sidewalk. He made my oldest brother get out of the car to help him. They found a piece of rope in the car and used it to tie the muffler up so it wouldn't drag on the road.

Mom didn't get home for three or four hours. I was a mess because I didn't know if she was ever coming back. My dad didn't say a word to her.

We never went to family therapy again.

One evening, after we finished eating dinner, my dad and my sister started to argue. My dad lost it and punched her in the face. He kept punching her, left, right, left, right. My oldest brother and my mom jumped on his back to stop him, but he dragged them through the dining room and through the kitchen until my sister was backed up against the kitchen wall.

Everyone was screaming, including me. I screamed at the top of my lungs, "Stop!"

My dad hit her with big roundhouse punches, left, right, left, right. I ran to the phone to call the police.

The phone was heavy and bulky and had a rotary dial. In order to call the police, you had to put your finger in the zero. If you dialed the zero before any other number, it connected you to the operator, and the operator would call the police for you. It took the longest time to dial the zero because it was the last number on the rotary dial, and I had to pull it all the way around. As the wheel returned, it made a rhythmic pulsing sound all the way back to the stop. It seemed like it was terribly loud, and I worried that my father would hear it and know what I was doing. Every time the operator picked up, I froze and hung up.

My dad will kill me if I call the police, I thought. I must have dialed five different times and hung up. I was terrified. At that time, we didn't have the technology for the operator to know where the call originated.

Finally, my dad stopped punching because he was winded.

The next day, my sixteen-year-old sister could not go to school because her face was so swollen. She looked like a professional boxer who'd lost a twelve-round fight. Her head was so swollen that the arms of her eyeglasses wouldn't fit over her ears.

My dad wasn't the only abuser. Both of my parents kicked, punched, and whipped us with extension cords and belts. They burned us with hot irons, poked us with knives and forks, broke broom handles over our backs, and more.

When I was thirteen, I'd had enough. I was upstairs in my room and had a knife from the Boy Scouts. I loved that knife. It had the BSA emblem on it and a wood finish that looked like the bark of a tree. The blade was sharp and ended in a point. I held that knife in my hand and cried for about an hour before I decided that I was going to kill myself.

Shaking and crying, I slowly pushed the blade into my abdomen. I must have pushed it three or four inches into my skin, but my skin just gave way. The blade would not pierce the skin. I was puzzled because the knife had a sharp point. I tried again, pushing it even deeper, but it would not break the skin. In hindsight, I believe God supernaturally intervened and saved me that day. Crying, shaking, and exhausted, I gave up. I put the knife on my dresser, curled up in a ball on my bed, and cried myself to sleep.

High School

When I was in high school, I discovered hard liquor and marijuana. I also discovered that I could sell marijuana to pay for my own stash of both. I had a reliable source for the pot: my sister. I'd buy an ounce of marijuana from her, clean out all the twigs and seeds, then roll joints, which I sold for a dollar. If I didn't know the person who wanted to buy, I'd tell them I didn't have anything to sell.

One time, however, I sold a joint to a friend of a friend. Just as we completed the transaction, a police car rolled by. We looked at each other in horror. The police must have seen our reaction because they hit the brakes and slowed down. I ran in the opposite direction down the one-way street, forcing them to drive all the way around the block. I turned the corner, ran halfway down that block, and laid on the street under a car. I stayed there for twenty minutes and prayed the owner didn't jump in the car and take off. Finally, I shimmied out from under the car, staying low until I could assess my surroundings. Then I stood up straight, acted like nothing special was going on, and sauntered casually down the sidewalk.

I wasn't exactly an honor student, but I made good grades and decided I wanted to go to college. My dream was to be a pastry chef in Manhattan. My love for baking came from the time I'd spent in the kitchen with my mom. Each year, she gave me more responsibility for the baked goods. At some point, I was doing all our baking for the holidays, and while I was immersed in flour and sugar, I found my true love.

A family with whom we were close friends had a son who'd graduated from the Cordon Bleu School in Paris, France. Brad was a chef in Manhattan. I told him about my dream, and he said that if he wrote me a letter of recommendation, I'd be accepted into the school. I replied that I was interested.

He then got in my face and said, "Listen, if I write you a recommendation and you decide not to go, my reputation will be tarnished. I'm going to give you thirty days to think about it. At the end of thirty days, if you say yes, you absolutely cannot back out. Do you understand what I'm saying?"

I wrestled with my decision. I wasn't even sure where Paris was. I didn't speak French. I was poor. How would I pay for flights, tuition, a place to stay, meals, and other necessities? I wanted this—really wanted it—but I knew I could not make a 100 percent commitment. At the end of the thirty days, I told Brad not to write the letter.

Young Adult

Instead, in the fall of 1977, I started my freshman year at Georgia Institute of Technology, a prestigious college located in the heart of Atlanta, Georgia. Being from metro New York City, I was glad I'd be going to college in a big city. Vic, a fellow classmate from high school, agreed to be my roommate. We were the first two students from our school to ever be accepted into Georgia Tech.

Vic had a nice car, a lime-green Dodge Charger with dice that hung from the rearview mirror. He picked me up early in the evening; his car was loaded down with all of our college stuff. We took off for Atlanta, a thirteen-hour drive. As the sun started to rise the next morning, we saw wide-open land. Vic and I were both shocked at the fields that went on and on until the horizon. We saw cows, something new for us. We agreed the next chance we got, we were going to pull off to the side and look at a cow. Off in the distance, there was a single, large cow standing next to the highway. Vic slowed down and stopped. I got out of the car.

"I think it's dead!" I shouted.

"What makes you think it's dead?"

"It is just standing here and not moving." I reached out and touched its head. It was the size of a baby's car seat. "I touched its head, and it didn't move. What should I do?"

"Knock on its head," Vic yelled back from the driver's seat.

He was about twenty-five feet away from me. I was nervous. The giant beast was held back by only two thin strands of barbed wire.

"Okay." I made a fist and knocked on its head like I would knock on a door. "I knocked, and nothing happened!" I shouted.

"Knock harder!"

I gave the cow a decent thump on its head, and it looked startled. It staggered for a few seconds, got its bearings, and gave me a look like it wanted to trample me.

I sprinted back to the car, yelling, "It's alive! It's alive!"

I jumped in the car, and Vic spewed gravel from beneath his wheels as we sped down the highway, screaming and laughing. Neither of us had ever seen a cow before.

As we moved into our dorm room, it was obvious to our neighbors that we weren't from Georgia. A big guy from across the hall must have been elected to come over and ask me if I was a Yankee.

"No," I said. "I like the Mets."

For all four years at school, the "Damn Yankee" stigma never let up.

I made new friends, and my drinking in college took me to a whole new level. It made high school drinking look mild. We would sneak Jack Daniels into the football games even though we'd arrived at the game already half drunk. We would buy sixteen-ounce "Coke Colas" in plastic Georgia Tech cups, take a big sip, top it off with Jack, and stir it with our index finger.

It was a busy few years. I ran track for the Georgia Tech Varsity Track Team: 110M high hurdles and 400M intermediate hurdles. I was a Lambda Chi Alpha fraternity brother. I worked twenty hours per week. I carried a full load of classes. I had a steady girlfriend during the last three years, and I managed to do all that while drinking, smoking pot, and taking uppers when I needed to study for a big test. It's incredible how much punishment a young body can take.

I graduated in 1981 with a bachelor's degree in industrial engineering and was offered two jobs. One was to be an industrial engineer at a Burlington factory in Burlington, North Carolina. It would have been a traditional industrial engineering role in a small town. The other offer from Florida Power and Light was in Miami, Florida. Having grown up in New York City, I was partial to the big city. So, I went to Miami.

About a year later, I went back to Atlanta to visit my sister and attend the Georgia Tech Homecoming football game. As we walked down the sidewalk, I ran into a friend I'll call Ann. She had dated one of my best friends and fraternity brothers while we were in school, so I knew her well. She was with another guy I'd never met before, and I assumed he was her boyfriend. We were headed in different directions, but we still managed to have a brief chat. She asked me for my phone number, and I gave her my business card.

A few weeks later, Ann called me at work. We reminisced about all the great times we had in college. Over the next few months, the calls intensified, and we agreed to meet halfway between Atlanta and Miami in Saint Augustine, Florida, for a long weekend. Saint Augustine claims to be the oldest city in the United States. It is a charming and beautiful city. We had a great time and were intimate. Things progressed, and nine months later, we were married. Almost as quickly, things went bad. In less than a year, we were separated, and two years later—when I was only twenty-seven—we were divorced.

I was having problems with my marriage, drinking too much, and craving cocaine. Most often, I bought cocaine from my friend's friend. I got to know him so well that I was in his apartment a couple of times. Let's call my friend Don and the cocaine dealer Jim.

One evening, I was out of cocaine. Once I started using it, I always wanted more, and when I used all the cocaine I had,

I got anxious and had to find more. But Jim didn't answer my repeated phone calls. I walked the few blocks from my condo to his apartment, the same complex where my friend Don lived. Jim wasn't home. And I *had* to have more cocaine.

Right out in the open, I started scheming about how to get into Jim's apartment. The complex was a grouping of single-story buildings with four apartments in each building. The way the property was laid out, you could see other buildings from your building. Oblivious to the neighbors, I decided to break into Jim's apartment.

His front door had about fifteen individual glass slats. On the inside, there was a crank that you would spin to open and close the glass slats—a common kind of door in South Florida, but not the most secure. After about thirty minutes, I removed a glass slat near the doorknob, reached in, and opened the door. I turned on every light in the apartment and searched everywhere for the stash of cocaine. I didn't find any.

I tried my best to leave everything as I'd found it. Dejected, I walked back home a guilty mess and crashed for the night. These were the times I would mentally beat myself up. I thought, *What is wrong with you? You stooped so low you broke into Jim's apartment. You need to stop doing this.*

A few days passed. There was a knock on my door, and I looked through the peephole to see Jim and Don. My guilt and my street-fighting instincts told me this was not a cordial visit. I opened the door and, in my most innocent voice, said, "Hey, what's up?"

Jim said, "Can we talk?"

I held my laundry basket and a few quarters and was in the process of heading to the building's laundry room.

"Sure. Walk with me to the laundry room."

The tension built. It felt like we were going to get into a physical altercation. As I shifted my wet laundry to the dryer, they tried to surround me and corner me. I maneuvered to keep both of them in front of me as I loaded another stack of dirty clothes into the washer. We made small talk. Before the tension could build too high, I broke the ice.

"Jim, I broke into your apartment."

They both seemed relieved that I'd said it first. The atmosphere shifted. I didn't know that Jim's neighbor had already told him about my break-in.

"What the hell did you do that for?" Jim said.

I explained myself. As I told the story, my eyes welled up, and I fought the urge to break down in tears. Both Jim and Don gave me a man-hug and said it was okay. I apologized to Jim and swore I didn't take anything and that I'd never do it again. As a cocaine dealer, Jim knew what people addicted to cocaine are capable of doing. We talked a little longer and laughed at what an idiot I was. I offered to pay for any damage to his door.

"Don't worry about it. We're good," he said.

Not long after, I was up all night, drinking and doing cocaine alone in my apartment. As I saw the dawn breaking, I realized I'd have to go to work in a couple of hours. There was no way I could go to work. I was a complete mess.

I freaked out. How could I call the office and act normal? Would my boss answer, or would his assistant answer? If the assistant answered, would my boss want to talk to me? Would I be able to speak intelligently? Somehow, I pulled it off. I called in and said I was sick, which meant that I had to lie. I didn't like lying to my boss.

I was disturbed that my addiction had now reached the level where I'd missed work. I sat on my sofa and stared at the wall in my one-bedroom condo. I felt like a complete failure and broke down in tears.

I was raised Catholic and had always heard that Jesus was at the door, and all I had to do was open it and ask Him in. I slid off the sofa and onto my knees. I folded my hands, bowed my head, and closed my eyes. I prayed as hard as I could.

"God, you say you're at the door, and all I need to do is invite you in. In my mind, I've opened the door and invited you in many times. But I don't feel like you've ever heard me or listened to me. God, come into my heart and do whatever you have to do to save my life. I'm either going to go to jail, or I'm going to die. God, do whatever you have to do! I completely surrender."

I knelt there and cried.

Don and I were such good friends that if either of our doors were unlocked, the other felt free to walk right in. Midmorning on a Saturday, I walked around the block to Don's apartment. It was a beautiful, sunny, south Florida day. I reached for the doorknob and burst in like Kramer on a *Seinfeld* episode and yelled, "Don!"

I clearly startled an attractive young lady who was making breakfast. Whatever she was cooking smelled incredibly good. The kitchen had an open floor plan and also had a counter coming out from the wall that separated the kitchen from the living room.

"Hello!" I said, "Who are you?"

"Who are you?" she replied.

"I'm Don's best friend."

We shared superficial information about ourselves and settled down. As I walked over to the fridge to grab a beer, I asked, "So where's Don?"

She didn't need to answer because Don walked out of the bedroom with bed head, a cup of coffee in one hand, and a lit cigarette in the other. He had a deep, raspy, I-just-woke-up voice as he laughed and made grumpy noises. Don was Italian, and he was loud. I'd known him long enough to know he was grumpy and made noises when he woke up. I understood that was his routine.

He finally said, "I need your help."

"What do you need?"

"I need you to get this beautiful woman to sleep with me."

Not too shocked that Don had asked such a question, I turned to her and asked, "Why won't you sleep with him?"

She said, "I'm a Christian, and I don't want to have sex before I'm married."

I let that sink in for a moment.

I looked directly at Don and said, "Buddy, you are on your own. I'm not arguing with that."

She smiled at me and asked me if I was a Christian. I was a little confused. I said, "I'm not sure what you mean."

She asked, "Do you believe in God?"

"Yes."

"Do you believe in Jesus?"

"Yes."

"Do you have a personal relationship with Jesus?"

Now I was stumped. I pondered her question.

Confused, I asked, "What do you mean by a personal relationship?"

She asked, "Do you want to have a personal relationship with Jesus?" She'd answered my question with a question.

Time slowed down. It's amazing how fast my brain can think when I feel like everything is slowing down. I thought, *I'm sitting here with an open beer between my legs. Can I ask Jesus to have a personal relationship with me with a beer between my legs? Do I believe in God? Do I believe in Jesus? Just the other day, I asked God to do whatever it takes to help me. Is this part of God's plan? I must believe in God if I asked for His help. But how do I have a personal relationship with a person who has been dead for over 2,000 years? This is crazy. She is waiting for an answer.*

A peace washed over me, and I calmly answered, "Yes."

She had a pan and wooden spatula in her hand. She froze and sort of snapped to attention like a soldier in the army whose officer shouted, "Atten-hut!" For a moment, she looked straight ahead and didn't move a muscle. I could tell her brain and her heart were working overtime. She put the pan and spatula down and walked toward me. The kitchen counter was just the right height for her to lean on, using her elbows to comfortably hold up her upper body.

She leaned forward and looked me in the eyes. "Will you say a prayer with me?"

I said, "Yes."

She bowed her head and closed her eyes. I thought I should do the same and bowed my head and closed my eyes.

"Repeat this prayer. 'Jesus, I believe you are the Son of God, and you died on the cross for the forgiveness of my sins.'"

I repeated, "Jesus, I believe you are the Son of God, and you died on the cross for the forgiveness of my sins."

She continued, "Jesus, I ask you to come into my heart. I want to have a personal relationship with you. Amen."

I followed, "Jesus, I ask you to come into my heart. I want to have a personal relationship with you. Amen."

As soon as I finished the prayer, I felt like a small bolt of lightning had hit me in the heart and taken my breath away. At the same time, in my mind's eye, I saw a drop of white paint dripped onto an infinite large black canvas. *Splat!* I looked up.

She asked, "Well, how do you feel?"

I said, "I feel like a bolt of lightning hit me in the heart."

She began to weep. Don, my tough-guy best friend from Jersey, began to weep.

I asked, "What is going on? Why are you both crying?"

Almost in unison, they said, "You've accepted Jesus, and your soul is saved."

That was in 1984, when I was twenty-five years old. I don't know that young woman's name, and I never saw her again in my life. What happened to me that day was supernatural. My life changed forever.

A few days later, I had a fight with my wife about our divorce and stormed out of my condo. I stopped and picked up a twelve-pack of beer. I drove from North Miami Beach to Coral Gables and everywhere in between. I was angry. I played the music loud, sang loud, cursed loud, slammed the beat out on the steering wheel. I was a mess. The empty beer cans piled up on the passenger floorboard. I was drunk, and I thought I needed to go home. I jumped on the Interstate, and about halfway there, I had an incredible urge to relieve myself. I started swinging my knees, opening and closing my legs. I tried with all my energy to hold it. *I can make it to my exit,* I told myself.

I got off the highway at my exit, 125th Street, a five-lane road with a turn lane in the center. As an engineer for Florida

Power and Light, I knew there was a substation just off the exit. There was a toilet in there, and I had a key. I swerved off the exit ramp. All I had to do was get to the first light and turn left. I raced toward the traffic light. There was a left turn lane with its own light. The light had a green arrow.

Yes! The green arrow switched to yellow. I hit the gas. The yellow light switched to red. I was still forty to fifty feet away. I pressed harder on the gas pedal and moved into the oncoming traffic lane to warn the drivers on the other side of the intersection that I was coming, and I wasn't stopping. The two oncoming lanes of traffic started to move toward me, and the drivers hit their brakes as I swerved around the left turn. I skidded to a stop on the gravel driveway right in front of the door to the substation. As I got out of my car, a police car with its blue lights flashing pulled up behind me.

I told them I had to go to the bathroom really badly and that I'd be right back. They looked at me with puzzled faces. I bet they thought, *This poor bastard is so drunk, he thinks this electrical plant fortress is a gas station. If he pees in public, we are going to have to add another charge.*

When I approached the door, I already had my key in my hand. *Boom!* I blew through the door as if it were unlocked. The room had a dirty feel to it. There was a desk with a few chairs. The desk and chair were there so that if a crew worked in the substation on a hot south Florida day, they could get some shade and complete their paperwork. The bathroom, well, it had a toilet and a sink. The sink was dirty with stains from many years of dirty hands being washed in it. The toilet was the same, clean but dirty, if that makes sense. The bathroom was dimly lit by a single incandescent light bulb.

I danced like a person being shocked by electricity. I jerked around so much, it was hard to get my zipper down. At last, I was peeing like a racehorse, a hard, steady stream hitting the water in the bowl like a fire hose. "Aaaahh," I sighed.

What am I going to do? I thought. *Maybe I could try to escape out the back of the substation. But my car is still out there.* I remembered an article I'd read that said to suck on a copper penny if you have had too much to drink and get pulled over. It had something to do with the interaction of the copper and the alcohol. I had two pennies in my pocket. I sucked on the pennies. I rinsed my face with cold water. *The cops are waiting outside. Maybe I could just stay in here. They can't get in. Oh no, not a good idea. They'll call Florida Power and Light, and then my employer would find out.* I worked up the courage to go back outside.

The officers didn't handcuff me, but they did tell me I was under arrest and that they would have to take me to the police station. I thought my life and my career were over.

I asked, "Where did you come from?"

They shouted, "You almost hit us as you cut us off!"

I said, "I didn't cut anyone off."

They laughed and said, "We were in the front row of cars at the light, and we thought you were going to plow into us."

The police station they worked out of was Liberty City. Two black police officers brought my white butt to the Liberty City Police Station at about 1:00 a.m. Being an engineer for FPL, I had to work all over Miami and had been to Liberty City many times to work on jobs, including when I supervised emergency crews at one o'clock in the morning. This was different; we had several large FPL trucks with their yellow lights flashing like the lights on a police car. Also, the people knew we were there to restore their power.

This time, I was in the back of a police car, arrested. I treated the police officers with respect, and they treated me with respect. We arrived at the police station with no issues. Even though every police officer I saw was black, they all treated me with respect. I blew 0.285 BAC on the breathalyzer. The legal limit was 0.10. I was at almost three times the limit.

By now, it was 2:00 or 3:00 in the morning. The Liberty City Police called my wife and told her I'd been arrested, and she needed to come and pick me up. She was not happy. First, I'd left earlier because we'd had a fight. Now, she got a call at 3:00 a.m., and a police officer asked her to come pick up her drunken husband. She had to drive alone into a predominantly black neighborhood at 3:00 a.m. She was angry when she arrived, and she yelled at me the whole way home.

I hired a good friend's father as my lawyer. We had to meet several times to plan our case. He was a long-time criminal defense lawyer. I can't recall what it cost, but I know it was between $2,000 and $3,000. That was a lot of money to me. He could not believe I'd still been conscious with a 0.285 BAC. I was so ashamed that I'd been driving with that amount of alcohol in my body.

The day came for my trial, and I had to tell my boss I needed to take off a day to go to court to plead not guilty for a speeding ticket. He could tell I wasn't telling him the truth. Over the course of a few days, he poked at me from many different angles.

"So, tell me again . . . you have to go to court for a speeding ticket? Why didn't you just pay it?"

I hated lying to him and wondered, *Will this ever end?*

My attorney told me to wear a suit. I was very nervous. It was a good thing I planned to get there early. I found the courthouse, and after I drove around the block several times, I parked my car. My attorney had told me which courtroom to go to, and to find a seat and wait to be called. The courthouse was big. The ceilings in the lobby had to be thirty feet high.

There were a lot of courtrooms. I found mine. I opened the door and saw that the room was packed. It looked like the United Nations in there. No one else was wearing a suit. I felt completely out of place. I saw a seat and had to climb over several people to get to it. We sat there as more people entered the room. People were wrapped around the interior walls, standing. People held the door open as the crowd grew in the hall. We waited. We all had to rise as the judge entered. She was a black female.

I thought to myself, *What are the odds that an overdressed skinny white boy who was arrested by two black officers would have a black female judge?* I felt sick to my stomach. I was certain I was going to jail.

One by one, the names of defendants were shouted out by a uniformed sheriff. Each person would stand up, make their way to the center aisle, walk down the aisle, and push open two miniature wooden swinging doors that were about three feet high. Those swinging doors were a nuisance. It almost felt like someone was playing a joke. People would have to lean down to open them. Maybe it was a way to force us to bow before the judge, who sat high up as if she was on a throne. It felt like she was ten feet above me.

"Mr. Bruce Sheridan!"

My mind raced. I sweated. Exhausted from worry, I felt terrible. When the officer yelled my name, I shot up like a rocket.

I may have even let out a quiet yelp. People followed me with their eyes as I made my way to the aisle. I saw my attorney standing at the defense table. I thought, *Where the heck did he come from?*

He smiled and held out his hand as if to say, "Come on up here; it's going to be okay." I thought I was going to faint. I had to get through the swinging wooden doors. My attorney and I stood as the judge flipped through a file in her hands. You could see she was getting increasingly agitated as she flipped through my file.

Finally, the judge slammed the file down. She looked at the prosecuting attorney with piercing eyes.

"Where are the arresting police officers?"

"Um, Your Honor, they were unable to make it."

"Where is form (blah blah blah)?"

"Um. Uh. I uh, I don't know, Your Honor," said the prosecutor as he fumbled around with his files.

The judge asked him several more questions. Her voice grew louder with each question. She took a deep breath and slowly exhaled. She smiled broadly at the prosecutor. I knew she was going to let him have it.

I thought, *What the fuck is going on? I can't believe the prosecutor has pissed the judge off so badly with my case. I'm definitely going to jail!*

In a loud voice, she said, "If you ever come into my courtroom again this ill-prepared for a case, you will regret it. Do I make myself clear?"

A red-faced, panicked prosecutor muttered, "Yes, Your Honor. It won't happen again."

The judge slapped the file closed, picked up her gavel, and gave it a good, hard whack, and proclaimed, "Case dismissed for lack of prosecution!"

My attorney put his arm around me and whispered in my ear, "In thirty-five years of doing this, I've never seen this happen."

His arm still on my shoulder, he slowly turned me around so that I faced the back of the courtroom. He whispered in my ear again.

"Son, you see those doors back there?" He pointed to the doors in the back of the courtroom. "You go through those doors, and you never look back."

With his hand in the middle of my back, he gave me a steady push until I started to walk away.

Still unsure of what had happened, I thought, *Am I going to be tackled by deputies and handcuffed?* My eyes darted around the room, looking for people in uniform. My breathing became more rapid. My heart raced. Adrenaline, what little I had left, began pumping. I walked out of the courtroom. No one tackled me.

I left the courthouse but, confused, I couldn't remember where I'd parked the car. The Miami sun pounded down on me. It was hot. I had to squint my eyes. My suit made me hotter. Where was my car? What had just happened? I couldn't think.

I finally found it and got in and removed the silver accordion cardboard from the windshield. I used it to block the sun from the dashboard and the steering wheel. Without that cardboard shield, I wouldn't be able to put my hands on the steering wheel until the air conditioning cooled off the car. I started the engine and turned on the air conditioner.

I put my hands on the steering wheel but was too emotional to drive. Then it hit me. I had asked God to do whatever He had to do to save my life. The DUI was *His* idea. I felt the Holy Spirit pour over me, and I began to sob. I sat in my car for twenty minutes, crying and thanking God. I thanked Him for doing whatever it took to save my life. There's no record that I was ever arrested. God saved my life!

> Now there was a Pharisee, a man named Nicodemus who was a member of the Jewish ruling council. He came to Jesus at night and said, "Rabbi, we know that you are a teacher who has come from God. For no one could perform the signs you are doing if God were not with him."
>
> Jesus replied, "Very truly I tell you, no one can see the kingdom of God unless they are born again."
>
> "How can someone be born when they are old?" Nicodemus asked. "Surely they cannot enter a second time into their mother's womb to be born!"
>
> Jesus answered, "Very truly I tell you, no one can enter the kingdom of God unless they are born of water and the Spirit. Flesh gives birth to flesh, but the Spirit gives birth to the Spirit. You should not be surprised at my saying, 'You must be born again.' The wind blows wherever it pleases. You hear its sound, but you cannot tell where it comes from or where it is going. So it is with everyone born of the Spirit."
>
> "How can this be?" Nicodemus asked.
>
> "You are Israel's teacher," said Jesus, "and do you not understand these things? Very truly I tell you, we speak of what we know, and we testify to what we have seen, but you people do not accept our testimony. I have spoken to you of earthly things, and you do not believe me; how then will you believe if I speak of heavenly things? No one has ever gone into heaven except the one who came from heaven—the Son of Man. Just as Moses lifted up the snake in the wilderness, so the Son of Man must be lifted, so that everyone who believes may have eternal life in him."
>
> For God so loved the world that he gave his one and only Son, that whoever believes in him shall not perish but have eternal life. For God did not send his Son into the world to

> condemn the world, but to save the world through him. Whoever believes in him is not condemned, but whoever does not believe stands condemned already because they have not believed in the name of God's one and only Son.
>
> John 3: 1-18

How could someone have written these words 2,000 years before that described what had happened to me—when I wasn't even sure what had happened to me? I walked into Don's house, and a woman I'd never met nor would see again asked me to pray a prayer to ask Jesus into my heart. A bolt of lightning hit me in the heart and took my breath away. A drop of white paint splashed on a black canvas. When the Holy Spirit washed over me after my case was dismissed, I was so overwhelmed I couldn't drive my car. My soul was born again. I was twenty-five but was now a baby in the Holy Spirit.

God had answered my prayer. I knew that I'd either be dead or in prison if I didn't get my act together. My soul craved the word of God, and I couldn't stop reading the Bible.

Don, my beer-drinking, coffee-in-one-hand, cigarette-in-the-other, two-and-a-half-packs-a-day best friend, was a Christian, and he attended Northwest Baptist Church. I was raised Catholic, so I wondered if I was allowed to go to a Baptist church. They had Sunday morning Bible study followed by Sunday morning service, Sunday evening service, and Wednesday evening service, and they expected you to attend all four. I'd have to go to church three times a week. That sounded crazy.

I knew that I'd either be dead or in prison if I didn't get my act together. My soul craved the word of God, and I couldn't stop reading the Bible.

Some of the things in the Bible sounded crazy, too. I began to realize that being a Christian was going to cramp my style. I also realized that I was a new man. The new me was beginning to believe that following the principles in the Bible was a recipe for living the best life.

God was patient, and I was stubborn. I didn't give in easily. I went to church Sunday morning, Sunday evening, and Wednesday evening. I loved it. Northwest Baptist Church had a large stage in front of the church, and the sanctuary was beautiful. I still remember the first time I sat in a service, and a large curtain rolled back. The associate pastor was standing behind clear plexiglass in about four feet of water. Parishioners came down a set of stairs and joined him in the pool. The pastor immersed them in the water, baptizing them. I thought, *What the heck is going on?*

I'd been baptized in the Catholic Church when I was a baby. A priest sprinkled water on my head. *That was good enough,* I thought. *I'm not walking into a pool and getting dunked in front of hundreds of people. No way, I'm not doing it.*

> Peter replied, "Repent and be baptized, every one of you, in the name of Jesus Christ for the forgiveness of your sins. And you will receive the gift of the Holy Spirit. The promise is for you and your children and for all who are far off—for all whom the Lord our God will call."
>
> Acts 2:38-39

What I learned and accepted is that being baptized is a personal choice. I couldn't make that choice when I was a baby. As an adult, I chose to be baptized in front of the congregation, and on June 23, 1985, pastor Bill Day baptized me in that pool.

I became involved in the youth ministry. I taught Sunday Bible study to high school students. I spent two to three hours a week preparing the lesson. I truly enjoyed teaching the high school students.

I stopped using drugs. Without the internet, it was not easy to find a meeting, but I figured out how to attend an Alcoholics Anonymous meeting. I was petrified to walk up the steps to the meeting the first time. *Am I supposed to pay? Is there a check-in? Are the coffee and cookies free? Holy cow, I recognize someone I know. It's Alcoholics 'Anonymous.' Am I allowed to act like I know him?* These thoughts and more raced through my mind.

It's a good thing there was a long stairway up to the meeting room because I was tempted to bolt out of there. Someone finally came up to me and greeted me. People welcomed me. By the time the meeting officially kicked off, there must have been forty to fifty people in the room. I recognized a few of the people and thought, *You can't tell who's had a problem with alcohol just by looking at them.* I thought everyone would look like a homeless, drunken bum. I was wrong. These were normal people.

I figured out that they passed around a microphone, and everyone took a turn. Just when I had begun to calm down, I again had the urge to run. Every person said, "Hello, I'm (name), and I'm an alcoholic."

The room would respond in unison, "Hello (name)."

Wait a minute, I thought, *I'm not sure I'm an alcoholic. Am I an alcoholic? I think I can handle my drinking. Do I have to say out loud, "Hello, my name is Bruce, and I'm an alcoholic?"*

As the microphone got closer, my heartbeat and breathing increased. I noticed that some people took the microphone and simply said, "Pass," and handed it to the next person.

That's what I would do. But after several meetings, I took the microphone and said, "Hello, I'm Bruce, and I'm an alcoholic." I had admitted I was an alcoholic. Wow!

I found a therapist, the same one who Don used. Her name was Nellie. I couldn't believe it. I, a tough, street-fighting New Yorker, was going to a therapist? I arrived about ten minutes early and sat in my car in the parking lot. I debated whether to go in.

During the first session, I asked, "How long will this take?"

Nellie said, "I don't know. Why don't we try three weeks and see how it goes?"

"Three weeks? Can't we finish this today?" I asked.

"No, I don't think so."

I wasn't happy with her answer. A three-week commitment? Was she crazy? Am I crazy? Every visit for those first three weeks, I asked her how much longer it would take. Nellie helped me, and I felt like our sessions were worthwhile. I eventually stopped asking how long it would take. In fact, I saw Nellie every week for four and a half years.

God was working on me, and he can work on you too.

My story is of a rough-and-tumble New Yorker who was headed for disaster. But God rescued me. He saved me from myself and put my feet on a better path.

Your story is different, but I imagine that we have a lot in common. As an emerging adult, I had a lot to learn about living a productive life. I'd never been taught how to survive, much less thrive in society, so with God's direction, I had to figure things out on my own. But you don't have to do that. In the following chapters, I'll share what I learned—all the hurdles and pitfalls and mistakes and disasters I had to overcome to become an adult. These lessons are for you too.

2

TAKE CONTROL OF YOUR FINANCES

Let's go back in time a bit. After my December graduation from Georgie Tech, I prepared to leave Atlanta and head to Miami for my first real job. I packed up my few belongings and contemplated what life would be like in Florida. I knew I wasn't going to have enough money. I owned two large Altec Lansing wooden box stereo speakers—thirty inches tall, twelve inches wide, and twelve inches deep. They were powerful and put out amazing sound. A friend of mine offered me $110 for them. Although it broke my heart to part with them, I needed the money.

I started working for Florida Power and Light (FPL) in January of 1982, and they had agreed to put me up in a hotel and let me use a company car to drive to and from work for the first few weeks before I got paid. I was forbidden from using the car for personal use. I could go to the grocery store or run necessary errands, but I'd be fired if I was spotted out on the town with the company car—a white station wagon with an FPL logo on the two front doors. Not exactly a sexy car or easy to hide.

The hotel was beautiful. It had a large pool and bar, and I could see the pool deck from my hotel room. Every day after work, I went for a swim, and on weekends, the pool area was crazy. There were lots of young people hanging around the pool and outdoor bar, but not many people were in the pool because it was winter in Miami. I'd come from temperatures in the teens and twenties in Atlanta. Sunny and seventy-five degrees felt like a heat wave to me. I enjoyed the pool immensely and had it all to myself. Every so often, when I got out of the pool, someone would say, "You do know it's winter, right?"

I wouldn't get paid for three weeks, and I was running out of money. I noticed that in the evenings, there were food trays outside many rooms that had uneaten food on them. I also noticed that the side dishes were served in metal serving dishes tightly wrapped with clear plastic wrap. I didn't have money to buy food, so one night, I grabbed a wrapped side dish and scurried back to my room. As far as I could tell, the broccoli had been untouched. After that, it was my daily habit to grab food from the trays. My favorite was a basket of sourdough rolls and a container of sour cream. I'd sit in my room, watch TV, and dip the rolls into the sour cream. Delicious.

I made the mistake of joking with people at work about eating off the trays, and a few days later, my supervisor, Mary, asked me if she could speak to me in her office. I thought I was in trouble. I sat across from her desk, and she closed the door. She leaned in on her elbows and folded her hands. Now I was certain I was in trouble.

Mary asked, "Is everything going well?"

"Yes," I replied.

"Is everything good at the hotel?" was her next question.

I thought, *Why is she asking me about the hotel? Did they complain to FPL? What an idiot. I'm broke. I traveled halfway across the country for this job. If I get fired, where will I go?*

I choked on my reply. "Yes. Everything at the hotel is okay."

"Are you sure?" she asked.

"Yes."

"Have you been eating food off of the trays in the hotel?"

Her question pierced me. I thought I was going to pass out. My life flashed before my eyes.

Mary rushed in to rescue me. I think she saw that I was going into shock. She rolled her chair back, reached in a drawer, and took out a sheet of paper. She slipped a check across her desk and turned it around so I could read it. It was made out to me in the amount of $400.

Still in shock, I searched for words. Nothing came out. I recovered my voice and asked, "What is this?"

"It's an advance on your pay," she said.

"I thought that was strictly against policy for new hires," I said.

Mary replied, "It is. But under these circumstances, I wanted to help you and got approval to give you an advance. Bruce, I want you to be comfortable coming to me about anything. If you are ever in a bind like this again, please let me know."

I couldn't believe this happened. I was stunned that she cared so much about me. I was rich! That was more than enough money to get me to my first paycheck. Mary arranged for FPL to take back $100 per pay period for the next four paychecks.

The paychecks kept coming. I got an apartment. I found a one-bedroom in Coconut Grove on Biscayne Bay, part of the intercoastal waterway. Coconut Grove, Florida, is a unique place. Pretty much every weekend, the town bustled. The Coconut Grove Arts Festival was a magnificent three-day event. It was so big that they had to shut down almost all the streets. Artists came from all over the world. It was fantastic.

I purchased a used diesel Volkswagen Golf that got fifty miles per gallon. Life was good. Then I opened the letter from the bank notifying me that I'd bounced a check. I couldn't believe my eyes. The one-page letter was cold, just the facts. "Check number 123, payable to ABC Company, returned for insufficient funds."

I'd bounced a check! *Screech!* I felt sick to my stomach. It was a wake-up call. I had to pay a fee to my bank as well as to the company that received the bad check.

I'd gone from eating food off the hotel trays to making $24,500 a year, and I spent money freely because I thought I was rich. However, I now had to be responsible. I was responsible for managing my money, keeping track of my checking account, and making sure that if I wrote a check, there was money in the account to cover it.

Recommendation:

Take responsibility for your money. Start by making a budget.

The graphic below shows a simple budget outline that you can use to get started. First, you need to write down all your sources of income and add up how much you expect to earn on a monthly basis. Second, you need to plan how much will be going out—how much you will spend. Simply put, the amount of money coming in needs to be greater than the amount going out.

LIFECOMPASS Budget October 20xx			
Income	**Monthly Income**	**Monthly Actual**	**Yearly**
Job 1	$AAA		$AAA x 12
Job 2	$BBB		$BBB x 12
Spending	**Monthly Budget**	**Monthly Actual**	**Yearly**
Giving	$ -		$ -
Saving	$ -		$ -
Rent/Mortgage	$ -		$ -
Utilities - Electric/Gas	$ -		$ -
Auto - payment, gas, repairs	$ -		$ -
Insurance	$ -		$ -
Cable/Internet	$ -		$ -
Mobile phone	$ -		$ -
Food	$ -		$ -
Medical	$ -		$ -
Clothing	$ -		$ -
Entertainment	$ -		$ -
Loans/Debt	$ -		$ -
Total	$ -		$ -

Figure 1: A budget outline

Debt Is Bad

What's this in my mailbox? Someone wants to give me a credit card? Yes! I thought. Well, it wasn't exactly as easy as that. I had to give them my life story first. I filled in the application, read the fine print, signed my name, and sent off the application. Weeks later, I received a letter declining me credit. I kept this up for months until, one day, I got a credit card. Dancing around my apartment with the card in my hand, I could hardly contain my excitement.

I was a great credit card customer. I carried a balance, charged above the credit card limit and paid a fee, was late on payments and paid a fee, and of course, I paid interest. I didn't care. I could buy things I wanted when I wanted, and I didn't need to have the money to buy them. How awesome is that? As it turned out, not so awesome.

Over time, the debt began to pile up. I was very careless when it came to my money. My bills would pile up on my kitchen table like my dishes piled up in the sink. I had the same philosophy for both. When the dishes piled up and fell over, it was time to do the dishes. When the bills piled up on my kitchen table and fell over, it was time to pay the bills.

I was a little embarrassed when I got my first collections call.

"Did you know your credit card bill is past due? When are you planning to pay it?" the representative asked.

I thought, *Are you calling me to pay my credit card bill when it's only one day past due?*

I was in the wrong but somehow felt like I wasn't. In addition to the late fees, interest charges, and other fees I was paying to use the credit card, now that it was in collections, it would negatively impact my credit score. So I made a plan to get rid of my debt. I consciously decided not to use my credit card to buy things. I forced myself to think, *Do I need this right now? Is it worth going into debt? Debt is bad.*

Credit cards are still a struggle for me. I recall wiping out our debt when we were selling one house and buying a new one.

The mortgage underwriter said, "You need to pay off all your credit card debt."

This meant we couldn't keep as much of the profit from selling our house because the lending bank insisted that we pay the $30,000 we owed in credit card debt. We were pretty upset.

I pushed back, "If we have a good credit rating and make our credit card payments on time, why do we have to pay off that debt?"

The underwriter said, "History and experience show that people who build up credit card debt will do it again and again. I can't approve the loan if you don't pay off the credit cards."

That felt like a punch in the stomach. I had been profiled as a credit card junkie. It turns out they were correct. Every time I got rid of my credit card debt, it slowly grew back. Like a monster, I had to wrestle it to the ground again.

Recommendation:

If you've never used debt, don't start. I strive to achieve a place where I give ten percent to God, I save twenty percent, and I live off of the seventy percent that is left over. It's a constant battle for me. But as a young adult, I'm telling you that it works. For each $100 you make after taxes, give $10 to God, put $20 in a savings account, CD, brokerage account, etc., and live off the remaining $70. Your life will be a lot less stressful life, and you'll be blessed by God.

There is only one topic in the Bible where God says to test him. That topic is about giving.

> "Bring the whole tithe into the storehouse, that there may be food in my house. Test me in this," says the LORD Almighty, "and see if I will not throw open the floodgates of heaven and pour out so much blessing that there will not be room enough to store it."
>
> Malachi 3:10

It took me decades to accept that everything comes from God, and all he asks is that I give back 10 percent. It's my pleasure to worship God with my giving.

Make Good Financial Decisions

Making good financial decisions is important, but it's not that easy. If you've never bought a car, or a house, or had a credit card before, how do you know what to do? Thank goodness for the internet. You can find an answer for almost any question you have. But unfortunately, even when you think you have all the answers, companies figure out new ways to take your money without providing value in return.

While I was an engineer for Florida Power and Light, I designed and oversaw the electric service installation for a two-story, thirteen-unit condominium in North Miami. I became good friends with the builder, Luis. Luis was a Cuban of below-average stature who spoke broken English and always had a big cigar in his mouth. He was probably in his fifties, and I was in my twenties. With my broken Spanish and his broken English, we somehow communicated. When the units were complete, Luis offered me a one-bedroom unit at a discount.

Buying that first home was frightening. I was going to make a commitment to pay $44,000 for a condominium in North Miami, Florida. I had no idea what I was getting into. I asked older people at work for advice. Every last one of them said I couldn't go wrong if I owned my own place versus paying

Making good financial decisions is important, but it's not that easy.

rent. Based on all the information I had, plus Luis helping me with the deal, I felt confident moving forward.

In hindsight, from the first day I moved in, there was an ever-so-slight downgrade in the neighborhood. I would even say it was undetectable. Undetectable but steady. Every day was a little bit worse than the day before. Ten years after I purchased my unit, 3,650 days later, the neighborhood was just plain bad. Throughout the previous six months, I heard occasional gunshots late at night. One evening, a SWAT team of about eight slammed open a neighbor's door with a big metal device. I came out to see what was going on, and they shouted, "Get back in your apartment!" They had automatic rifles and black jackets with the big white letters *FBI* on their backs. I went back to my unit and didn't come out until morning. I had to sell the unit.

I lost $16,000 when I sold it. The first three years of my thirty-year mortgage, I'd had a negative amortization loan, which allowed me to have a lower monthly payment so I could afford the condo. Negative amortization meant I didn't pay enough each month to cover the interest and principal payment. The amount I didn't pay was added back into the amount of the loan, and after three years of paying my mortgage, I owed the bank more than the original loan amount. Combine that with the value of the property going down from day one, and I owed the bank $16,000. I sold my condo for $22,000 with a mortgage of $38,000 on the property. I literally cried when I realized that I'd held real estate for ten years and sold it for half the amount I paid for it. It wasn't supposed to work that way. But I wanted to buy the condo, and the negative amortization loan sounded fine to me, as long as I could afford the monthly payments. The fact that I wasn't building any equity and was, in fact, increasing the amount I owed on the condo never occurred to me.

Over the past thirty-one years, my second wife and I have purchased and sold seven homes. On every home, we've made tens of thousands of dollars. When you buy a home, you have to pay attention to many variables. For example, on the last home we sold in 2019, the buyer's real estate agent tried to make us pay $15,000 for a new roof. He even went so far as to charge us the $15,000 on the closing documents hours before the closing. She hoped we wouldn't notice and would sign the papers. Of course, we didn't sign.

There will always be people out there trying to take your money without providing value in return. Find mentors, friends, and family you can trust to have your best interests at heart, and always seek their advice before making major financial decisions.

I can't promise that you'll make it through life without being taken advantage of. What I can tell you is that if it sounds too good to be true, be wary. There are few for-profit companies that will make a deal with you that makes them lose money. "For-profit" means they're trying to maximize their profit. They can't do that by helping you out, despite what they say about the customer always coming first. The truth is their bottom line comes first.

Recommendation:

You need money to live and to pay your bills, but be careful not to make money more important than God or the people you love.

> For the love of money is a root of all kinds of evil. Some people, eager for money, have wandered from the faith and pierced themselves with many griefs.
>
> But you, man of God, flee from all this, and pursue righteousness, godliness, faith, love, endurance and gentleness. Fight the good fight of the faith. Take hold of the eternal life to which you were called when you made your good confession in the presence of many witnesses.
>
> 1 Timothy 6:10-12

I have many examples I could give you about the inner workings of our financial system, but I'll only share one. When I was at Bank of America, the CEO asked all business unit leaders to figure out how to pump up profit in the fourth quarter. That was not an easy task. It was September, and that didn't give us a lot of time to figure it out, let alone implement the solutions.

I was asked to sit in on an all-day meeting on the credit card business to brainstorm how to bring in more profit. At the time, credit cards generated $5 billion in profit for Bank of America.

Our credit card customers who paid their balance in full and were never late or over their limit thought they were our best customers. But they were actually our worst customers when it came to profitability. We like the customers who were late because they paid a $35 late fee. A customer who went over their limit also paid a $35 fee. If they did this more than once in a twelve-month period, we increased their interest rate to over twenty percent. That was good.

We spent about an hour figuring out how we could squeeze more money out of the paid-in-full, never-late, never-over-limit customers. They had twenty-eight days to pay their bill. They didn't know it, but we actually gave them twenty-nine days. If they paid late, we didn't feel bad about charging them the late fee because they had twenty-eight days, plus an extra day to pay.

Someone asked, "Can we give them less than twenty-eight days to pay?"

We didn't know the answer. We called our assigned attorney to meet with us. All the attorneys were on alert and knew we were working on profit ideas for the CEO. Our attorney showed up within thirty minutes.

"Can we give this group of customers less than twenty-eight days to pay?" we asked.

"When a customer uses the card," the attorney said, "they agree to our terms and conditions. In the terms and conditions, we stipulate we can assign between seven and twenty-eight days to pay."

Our next question was, "Do we have to notify them if we shorten the twenty-eight days to seven days?"

"No, it's in the agreement," he said. "As long as you stay within the seven to twenty-eight days, a notice isn't necessary."

So we changed the rules. We told the phone representatives that if any of these customers called, we would apologize and refund the late fee. We figured that about 15 percent would call to complain. I can't recall how much profit it generated, but it was an impressive amount.

The lesson here is to watch your money closely and avoid debt whenever possible.

And while we're on the subject of money, let's talk about how to get it. We'll do that in Chapter Three.

3

UNLESS YOU'RE RICH, GET A JOB

I started work when I was ten years old. I delivered the *Hudson Dispatch* newspaper to roughly eighty homes, Monday through Friday. My brother, Mark, who's three years older than me, had a paper route, and I wanted one too. The manager asked me to come in with my brother at 5:30 a.m. What—5:30 in the morning? That seemed ridiculous to me, a ten-year-old boy.

The first day, the manager said, "Wait over there," and he pointed to a corner. I saw stacks of papers everywhere. It was a small storefront under an apartment building just off Summit Avenue, a main street. It wasn't an impressive place, but it didn't need to be. In the middle of the night, the newspaper company dropped off the papers, and at about 5:00 a.m., the manager showed up and prepared individual piles.

Older boys arrived, folded their papers into tomahawks, loaded their bags, and took off. It was a mad rush and lasted about twenty-five minutes. Then it was just the manager and me. He asked me a lot of questions. One question was how old I was. In two months, I would be eleven, so I told him I was eleven. He asked me when my birthday was.

I said, "In two months."

In his mind, I was eleven now and would be twelve in two months. Not exactly the truth. To be honest, I didn't know you had to be twelve years old to deliver the papers, and I didn't know what he was thinking. I got the job even though I was only ten.

When the manager found out my real age, he said, "I shouldn't let you have a route, but your brother is good, and I assume you will be too. I'm going to keep an eye on you."

The other paper boys used the tomahawk fold because if you threw the paper with a high enough arch, when it hit the ground, it would unfold as if you had taken the time to walk it to the door and lay the paper down. I got good at the tomahawk fold and throwing the paper accurately. I learned to be accurate after crawling around in the bushes after accidentally throwing the paper into them. I only had fifteen houses where I needed to throw the paper, so I put all my papers into my heavy-duty canvas bag and loaded the fifteen folded ones on top. The bag sat up on a table. The older boys could just strap the bag over their shoulders, but I wasn't strong enough. I had to duck down and come up through the space between the bag and the strap. I'd put the strap on my forehead and then lean forward until the bag came off the table and rested in the small of my back. Leaning forward the whole time, I marched off to my first house.

After I got rid of about twenty papers, I could carry the bag over my shoulder. Every paper I delivered made the bag lighter and more manageable. When I was done, I hurried home, grabbed my book bag, and raced off to school. I was allowed to walk in through the front door of the school because I was a working man. I could be late as long as it wasn't excessive. Every once in a while, I'd see the principal and salute him as my heart burst with pride. He would smile and acknowledge me. At ten years old, I was a working man.

After that first week, I was tired and exhausted. Being at the newspaper office at 5:30 a.m. and then rushing around delivering papers was hard work. I got bad news from my father after my first week of work.

"How much did you make?" my dad asked.

"Ten dollars."

My dad said, "That's great. You need to give me $1.50."

I couldn't believe my ears. In disbelief, I asked, "Why do I have to give you $1.50?"

He said, "Fifteen percent room and board."

I gave him the $1.50. I was upset, but I kept quiet because I knew better than to push back.

I had many jobs between being a newspaper boy and my first real job. I painted, refinished gym floors, worked construction, and provided security at a high-end condominium, to name a few.

My title in Miami at Florida Power and Light Company was "Energy Conservation Specialist." The demand for power in Florida was so great that Florida Power and Light was willing to pay a portion of the expense for its customers to upgrade their homes and use less electricity. Imagine a company trying to get people to buy less of their product. My job was to go to homes and businesses and encourage them to put UV blocking film on their windows, add insulation in their attics, and upgrade their old air conditioners.

Starting work at age ten and working my way through college had given me a good work ethic. In nine months, I was promoted to the Power Grid Engineering and Construction Training Program. I loved it. I got to design and oversee the construction of electrical power into homes and buildings. After FPL completed a large residential subdivision project, I went back at night to drive through. There were probably three hundred homes. I drove slowly as I watched families in their homes and front yards and thought to myself, *I played a big part in getting the electricity to these homes.* It felt good.

About two to three years in, I thought, *I wonder if I should get another job.* I was a little bored and wanted to do something different. I scratched out a resume by hand and then typed it on a typewriter. There were no word processors in those days. I had to buy paper, feed it through a roller on the typewriter, make sure it was lined up properly, and then begin typing. As the line of type approached the right edge of the paper, a bell rang. There was a silver metal arm sticking out at the top that I'd push to the right, which automatically advanced the paper to the next line. Making a mistake was brutal. It meant I had to throw away the paper and start over.

When I finally had a version of my resume that I liked, the next step was to buy nice paper and matching envelopes. At the office supply store, I selected an off-white paper. I was friends with a printer in town. I brought him my resume, and we struck a deal to print fifty resumes. They'd be ready in a few days.

A couple of days later, I walked into the trailer that now housed our offices. Our department had moved from the second floor of the customer service branch out to the service center. Mary thought we needed to be close to our crew members, who belonged to a big union, the International Brotherhood of Electrical Workers (IBEW).

Before I could sit down at my desk, Mary called to me.

"Can I see you in my office for a minute?"

I got that same feeling in my stomach as when she called me in to ask me if I was eating food from the trays at the hotel. Whenever Mary asked, "Can I see you in my office for a minute?" it meant she was serious. Mary was not in a joking mood.

"Have a seat," she said as she closed the door.

I wondered why she was closing the door.

Mary continued, "How's everything going?"

Oh no, not that question again. I replied, "Great."

"Do you like your job?"

I wondered, *Is she going to fire me? Why is she asking me if I like my job?* Trying to act calm and collected, I said, "I love my job."

"So, you love your job? Is there anything about your job you're unhappy with?"

The voice in my head began talking to me: *What's going on? Why did she close the door? Why is she asking me these questions? Stay calm. Don't freak out.*

I said, "You know I love my job. I enjoy designing the systems, watching the crews build the power grid, and seeing a finished product. When a job is done, I think to myself, 'I built this!'"

Mary rolled her chair back and opened the thin drawer in front of her. She was unnervingly quiet. She pulled out a single piece of paper, flipped it around so I was able to read it, and slid it across her desk as she said, "Well then, what is this?"

It was my resume. It was printed on the expensive colored paper I'd bought. I stared at it, hoping it would change right before my eyes. I hadn't even picked up my resumes from the printer yet.

"How did you get this?" I asked.

With a smirk, Mary said, "The printer is my neighbor."

My immediate thought was, *That bastard. If I get fired, I'm going to sue him.* Mary could tell my New Yorker attitude was boiling up inside me. I was speechless. I was getting angry, and my facial expression showed it. I squirmed in my seat. It felt hot in the room. *Hold it together; you cannot lose it at work,* I thought.

Mary broke the silence, "Don't worry. You're not in trouble. You can look for a job any time you want. You're an outstanding employee, and I don't want to lose you."

I started to calm down, but I wasn't sure I believed her.

"If there's any job you want here at Florida Power and Light, I want to try to help you get that job."

That was a quick reversal. I thought I was going to be fired, but now she wanted to keep me and help me. I replied, "Any job?"

"Yes, any job."

After a long pause, I replied, "Well, there is a job I would like. I know the Southern Division is considering expanding the rollout of the Quality Improvement Program. I would love to work on that."

"Great," she said. "I'll see what I can do."

I returned to my desk a nervous wreck. That incident had sucked the life out of me. I couldn't get my mind to focus. I was still pissed off at the printer, but I had to get back to work. Due to the nature of our job, we went out into the field in the middle of the day. I needed to get out.

I returned to our trailer around 2:00 p.m. Mary greeted me, and she seemed excited.

"Can I see you in my office?" she asked as she speed-walked ahead of me. Mary seemed to have a surge of energy in her step.

She closed the door. Before she even sat down, she said, "Do you own a suit?"

"Yes."

"Good. You need to wear your suit and be down at the Southern Division office tomorrow at 8:00 a.m. You have an interview with the Southern Division VP."

I had to leave my house by 7:00 a.m. to get to the Southern Division office and be comfortably settled by eight o'clock. The executive suite intimidated me. Each executive had an oversized office. Just outside each office, an assistant sat at an L-shaped desk with an electric typewriter. There was a waiting area with a television, upscale furniture, and newspapers and magazines neatly placed on end tables. I sat in my chair and waited to be called. Just twenty-four hours ago, my boss had managed to get my resume, and here I was, waiting to be called in to speak with the vice president of the largest division in the company. The interview went well.

I got back to the trailer mid-morning. Mary was waiting for me.

"Can I see you in my office?" The happy "Can I see you in my office?" was different from the stern "Can I see you in my office for a minute?" This was a happy request.

She closed the door and sat down at her desk. In a serious, stern voice, she asked, "What the hell happened down there at the Southern Division office?"

I had been beaming, a big smile on my face. Now my face fell. I couldn't help but think, *Oh no! What did I do now? I thought the interview went well. I don't think I did anything wrong. Is this happening?*

I mustered up my confidence and said, "I thought the interview went pretty well."

Mary couldn't hold it in anymore. She became super-giddy and said, "The VP wants you to report at the Southern Division office at 8:00 a.m. Monday."

I felt like I'd just won a million dollars. We celebrated together in her office. The big smile was back on my face.

Once more, God had intervened in my life. Thursday morning at 8:00 a.m., my boss had my resume in her hands, and I thought I was about to be fired. Twenty-four hours later, the Southern Division Vice President, one of the top ten executives at the company, was interviewing me. Monday morning at 8:00 a.m., I was to report to the VP in a new role. Those three days turned my world upside down and would change the trajectory of my career forever.

The Southern Division office was located at West Flagler Street and South LeJeune Road in Miami. It was a secure building. There was a live guard you passed to enter the building, which was a little intimidating. My boss was Clark Cook. His boss was Larry Adams. Larry reported to the CEO, John Hudiburg. Their three personalities could not have been more different. John was quiet. Larry was loud. Clark was polished. Together they were a balanced team.

My role was to figure out how to implement a comprehensive system to set the Southern Division's strategic plan, create a quantitative dashboard, teach employees from top to bottom how to identify the root cause of their issues and solve problems, teach leaders how to manage by the strategic plan, and hold middle managers accountable for results. In addition, we had to work with the IBEW union, satisfy customers, improve safety, maintain a positive relationship with the Florida Public Service Commission, and hold our suppliers accountable.

It was my dream job. I didn't care that no one knew what to do with me when I showed up on Monday or that I landed in a small, windowless office on the other end of the building. I was still on the top floor of the Southern Division headquarters, and I was hanging out with the executive team.

Recommendation:

Mary and Clark were two of the best bosses I've ever had. Mary was polished, quick, and "wicked smart," as we say in the northeast. Clark was a people person, well-mannered, a gentleman. They both loved me, and I loved them. Finding that in a boss is not common.

I urge you, plead with you, to take control of your career. You will have people in your life who will hurt your career, and you will have people in your life, like Mary and Clark, who will help you. But you have to take responsibility for your career yourself. Think about what you are great at and love to do. You should spend the majority of your time in pursuit of that sweet spot.

You're going to spend the majority of your waking hours wrapped around a job, so I recommend that you find one that you love. I figured out that few people were going to be concerned about my career. They have enough going on in their own lives. They can't take on the burden of figuring out my career, and it's not their responsibility anyway. So, don't simply expect things to happen. You have to take responsibility for your career.

If You're Stuck—Run!

In my ninth year of work at Florida Power and Light, we got a new CEO, James Broadhead. Being the new mayor in town, he shook things up a little. He brought in his own team and was going to change the company structure. Broadhead announced we were not going to waste time on the Quality Improvement Program. In addition, he brought in Booz Allen Hamilton consulting firm to review operations from top to bottom.

I had spent seven of my last nine years working to help build the Quality Improvement Program. Now the new CEO said it was a waste of time. That was a punch in the gut. We'd saved close to $500 million. We'd set up a structure to cascade the goals from top to bottom. We'd taught employees how to work in teams and solve problems at the root. We'd filed several patents. We were the first non-Japanese company in the world to win the Deming Prize for quality. We were called in by the United States Congress to create the Malcolm Baldridge National Quality Award.

James Broadhead had the NIH syndrome, the "Not Invented Here" syndrome. His predecessor created the Quality Improvement Program, but his ego told him the Quality Improvement Program had to go.

I hold a Bachelor of Science and a Master of Science in Industrial Engineering. My manager at the time, José Alvarez, holds a Bachelor of Science and a Master of Science in Industrial Engineering and was an Industrial Engineering Adjunct Professor at the University of Miami. For the past four years, I had worked as an industrial engineer in FPL's Management Services department. Ninety percent of the people in the department were industrial engineers, so you could have called it the "Industrial Engineering" department, and you would have been correct.

Booz Allen Hamilton was, and still is, a nationally recognized management consulting firm. One of their greatest strengths was industrial engineering. Booz Allen Hamilton made its way through the company looking for departments to cut. The more they cut, the more impressed the CEO would be, and the CEO could use some of the savings to give Booz Allen Hamilton a nice, juicy consulting contract. Booz Allen Hamilton recommended that the entire Management Services Department be eliminated. That was gut-punch number two.

José and I still stay in touch. He was another great boss in my career. José said, "When Larry Kelleher came and had a meeting before the 1992 major reorganization and said Management Services would not exist and that none of our jobs would exist, that was a big jolt for all of us. We were part of a stable utility and were part of a department that had recently been instrumental in winning the Deming Prize. The good thing was that the line departments valued our skills and picked us up in leadership and analyst positions."

My recommendation is to not look at others and wish you had their career. Take charge of your career, knowing the road will be bumpy. But at least you are driving the car.

I had a gut feeling the new CEO was going to shake things up. I didn't know he was going to shut down my department and the program to which I had dedicated the majority of my career. I got nervous and started to send out my resume to a few select companies. It paid off. In January 1991, I landed a job in Charlotte, North Carolina, at Southern Pump and Tank Company (SPATCO).

SPATCO was comprised of three divisions. The Petroleum Division could build or tear down gas stations with convenience stores. The Liquid Process division sold pumps, tanks, and control systems to chemical plants. The Environmental Division cleaned up liquid spills and contaminated ground water.

Sandy was the head of Human Resources. I was hired as the Director of Total Quality Management. One of the first things I did was set up a two-day workshop with all the senior managers of the company.

As part of the workshop, I wanted to get the team out of the office and have them do something fun. Sandy and I went to a local college to visit their outdoor team-building facility. They had a fifteen-foot wall the team would have to climb over. There was a trust fall, a ropes course, and several other activities that required physical skills and teamwork to solve problems. It was in a wooded area, and when Sandy and I left, I started to drive out of the woods. The road ended, and I began to drive through what could only be called raw woods. The terrain got so bad, I got nervous. So did Sandy.

Sandy said, "Bruce, seriously, we need to get out of here."

I can't tell you why I did what I did next. I think because Sandy was so nervous, I thought it would be funny. I replied, "My real name isn't Bruce," with a serious look on my face.

Sandy got more nervous but tried not to show it. "You're full of shit. Your name is Bruce, and you are engaged to marry Jan."

In a calm voice, I replied, "There is no Jan. I made that up."

Sandy got so upset, she jumped out of the car and started running through the woods. I freaked out. I'd only been on the job a month or two, and I'd just creeped out the Director of Human Resources.

I jumped out of the car and yelled, "Sandy, I was kidding!" It took me a few minutes to convince her I wasn't a psychopath trying to kill her. I gently coaxed her, and she got back in the car. I apologized several times. I tried to back my car out of the woods and almost got stuck. By the time we got back to the office, we were laughing. She was still upset with me, but we couldn't stop laughing. We worked together for two years in a great partnership, teaching and coaching the leaders of the company.

Recommendation:

Do your best to work with people you enjoy. Life is too short to work with people with whom you don't get along. There's a company out there where you will fit right in. Have the courage to embrace the truth that you deserve to work at a place where you fit in. Have the courage to look for another job if you need to.

Some people spend thirty-five years at one company, and others move from job to job and city to city. I often hear people say they wish they'd done the opposite of whatever they chose. Lesson learned. People think the grass is greener on the other side. My recommendation is not to look at others and wish you had their career. Take charge of your own career, knowing the road will be bumpy but that at least you're the one driving the car.

Try to Pick a Good Boss

I've had some great bosses, and I've had some bad bosses. The physical and mental toll of a bad boss can be devastating. If you have a miserable boss, both your work life and personal life can be miserable. My friend is a doctor, and he told me, "Bruce, more than half the patients I see don't have a disease. Their symptoms are from stress."

If you have a miserable boss, both your work life and personal life can be miserable.

CitiMortgage, a unit of CitiBank, was located in O'Fallon, Missouri, a suburb of Saint Louis. CitiMortgage recruited me for months. I'd lived in Charlotte, North Carolina, for thirteen years and had a son going into his senior year of high school and two sons at North Carolina State University. I didn't want to move. After months of back and forth, in 2012, Citi offered me a senior role that sounded exciting. The salary was great, and Citi agreed to pay 100 percent of my relocation expenses.

I'll call my manager Manny and his manager George. On my third day on the job, George, who was a senior executive from Manhattan, called me into his O'Fallon office, which was in the corner of the top floor of the campus. It was the executive wing, isolated from the rest of the workers. In the interior of the executive suite, there was a large pool of executive assistants. I got two steps into the executive suite, and one of the assistants began to interrogate me.

"Hello, how may I help you?" was what she asked, but the way she looked at me said, "Do you belong here? Because I have never seen you before. Shoo, go away! You appear to be lost."

"I'm here to see George," I told her.

"Oh. Can I tell him who's here?"

"Bruce Sheridan."

"Please have a seat, and I'll let him know you're here."

I was led to George's office. He got up, walked past me, and shut his door. On his way back to his desk, he asked, "How are things going so far?"

We made small talk for a few minutes. George paused, resettled himself in his seat, leaned in, and said, "I wanted to ask you a question."

"Yes."

"Why do you think you were hired?"

I thought I'd already passed the interview. It was only my third day with the company. My first day was an all-day orientation, and my second day was to meet my team and settle in. Why did George ask this question? I thought with all my brain power and gave him the best answer I could.

"I was hired to reengineer the mortgage process from application to loan paid in full. I'll work with the various department heads to identify low-hanging fruit and simplify and improve our processes. After that, we'll dig deeper and solve more complex problems. My goal is to increase revenue, reduce expenses, mitigate risks, and ensure regulatory compliance." Pleased with my answer, I sat back and waited for George's approval.

"Nope! Why do you think you were hired?" he asked a little more powerfully, and his posture became slightly more aggressive.

I prepared to give George a better answer than the first one. I'm pretty sure my second answer was a tad bit longer than the first answer. I tried to hit harder on the key points I'd just mentioned. I thought for sure George would be pleased with this answer.

As I spoke, George sat back and let me go on, almost as if he wasn't listening. His attitude almost shifted to whimsical, as if he was now enjoying being a jerk.

When I finished my answer, he looked me straight in the eyes and said, "Nope! Why do you think you were hired?" He leaned forward on his desk and gave me his full attention, and stared into my eyes as if to say, "Please don't be stupid enough to give me the same answer again."

Now I was starting to get upset. *What kind of bullshit is this? My third day on the job and my manager's boss is grilling me. What is going on?* ran through my head.

I replied, "Well, obviously, I don't know why I was hired. Would you care to enlighten me?"

Now I had hit the bullseye. George leaned forward and said, "You were hired because we told Manny that if he hired another Indian, we'd fire him."

It felt like a flash grenade went off right in front of me. I was blinded, and my ears were ringing. Had he just said what I thought I heard?

It's amazing how fast your brain can process when it is in shock. That explained why I got such a great salary. That explained why I was extended the offer to lead the department. That explained why I was given a full relocation package when they hadn't given one to a new hire in five years. I thought I was going to throw up.

I soon realized that I was at the same pay grade as my manager, Manny. Citi did not need to pay both of us to do the same job. Within the first two weeks, Manny informed me I would only be managing a third of the department. The third of the department I managed was all the non-Indian teammates.

Manny also instructed me not to speak to senior executives. That was his job.

> Whatever you do, work at it with all your heart, as working for the Lord, not for human masters, since you know that you will receive an inheritance from the Lord as a reward. It is the Lord Christ you are serving. Anyone who does wrong will be repaid for their wrongs, and there is no favoritism.
>
> Colossians 3:23-25

The only way I could get through the day was to pray and remind myself that I worked for the Lord. I tried as hard as I could to work with other executives to reengineer the mortgage process from the point where a customer was considering a mortgage to the point where they paid off their mortgage. If they were buying a new house after paying off their mortgage, we needed to do our best to keep their business. None of my peers or other department heads would give me the time of day because they did not like, nor trust, Manny. Quicken Loans, now Rocket Mortgage, was crushing Citi Mortgage. Rocket Mortgage was fast, their processes were superior, and they won the J.D. Power customer satisfaction award year after year. It frustrated me that my hands were tied.

After four months, I was called into the Human Resources office and told I was being fired and that I had to fire my team. About ten people reported directly to me. Manny also had about ten direct reports. In addition, Manny had about ten consultants from India through Tata Consulting. Most of them lived in India and were here on work visas, staying in a hotel paid for by CitiBank. None of Manny's team or any of the Tata Consultants were let go, but my entire team was let go. I could not understand why ten consultants were retained, and my team and I were fired.

One at a time, I called my team members into my office and told them the company no longer needed their services. Firing my team was one of the most horrible things I've ever done in my career. Through tears, anger, and disappointment, each person left the office in shock.

What was I going to do? I'd moved my family to St Louis. I'd uprooted my third son, and he was attending a new high school for his senior year. My second son had just completed his freshman year at North Carolina State University, and he'd had to transfer to the University of Missouri because I couldn't afford to pay out-of-state tuition at NC State. My youngest had to start his freshman year of high school in a new city. My wife and I had spent thirteen years in Charlotte and had left many dear friends behind. Now four months into my new job in St Louis, I had lost it.

Recommendation:

Taking responsibility for your own career is a never-ending journey. Throughout life, no matter what you choose as your vocation, you'll have to deal with other people and, most likely, someone in authority over you.

There are two types of authority: position authority and moral authority. An extreme example of position authority is the military. When someone with a higher rank tells you to do something, you are going to do it. You can't quit. An extreme example of moral authority is someone in your life or family, or a friend, mentor, boss, etc., who you believe in. This person has a moral code that they exemplify and live by, and you completely respect them and want to be like them.

When you take a job with a company, you agree to submit to people with position authority. Most likely, you'll have a boss, and they'll have a boss. Anyone higher up in the company could impact your career. Occasionally, people at your level or even lower may have more authority than you. For example, the owner's son or daughter may be at a lower level than you but don't for one moment think you have more authority. If the son or daughter decides they don't like you, you could be out the door. The main thing I want you to know is that if you have a miserable boss, your work life and personal life can be miserable.

If you think things might change over the next six to twelve months, you might want to hang in there. The outcomes I've experienced are that my miserable boss quit, my boss got moved to another role, or I got moved to another role. If you don't think things will change, find a new job.

As I mentioned in Chapter One, I came from a physically and verbally abusive family. It's not something you walk away from without scars, and I'm talking about emotional and mental scars rather than physical ones. In the next chapter, I'll tell you how I dealt with the fallout from the abuse.

4

ABUSE IS FOR COWARDS

I was number four of six children. We were an Irish Catholic family. The Catholic Church took the Bible verse "go forth and multiply" seriously. My mom finished high school, but my dad quit school at sixteen after his freshman year. He was the oldest of eight children and had to work to help support the family. My father's father, my grandfather, was a tough man. My grandfather physically abused my grandmother and the entire family.

My father told me he came home one day, and his dad was hitting his mom.

"I came into the house and heard my dad screaming at my mom, and he was hitting her. I'd had enough. I pulled him off my mother and punched my father in the face so hard, I knocked him out. I broke his nose and caused him to partially lose hearing in one ear."

That story astonished me. I wondered, *If my father hated the abuse from his father, why did he abuse us?* Later in life, my therapist would explain to me that the cycle of abuse is hard to break. Just like my father got tired of being abused by his father, by the time I was in high school, I was tired of being abused by mine.

When I entered high school in 1973, I was tall and skinny. When I was a few years younger, there was a Joe Weider gym two short blocks from my house. It was a one-story building on a corner lot. Seeing bodybuilders going in and out all day piqued my interest. A few friends and I tried to peek in the windows, but a big guy came outside and yelled at us. We ran away as fast as we could. We were so scared that we wouldn't look in the window for months. But we always managed to be lured back to get a look at the bodybuilders.

I must have been eight years old when I worked up the courage to walk into the gym. The men were gigantic, muscles bulging out everywhere. They lifted heavy weights, made all kinds of loud noises, and then dropped the weights, crashing them to the floor, which shook the whole building. I couldn't discern what the smell was, but it smelled bad in there.

One of the bodybuilders noticed me watching in awe. He pointed me out and called to the manager. Another giant man approached me. He tried to catch his breath as he wiped sweat off his brow. With a big smile on his face, he said, "What can I do for you, kid?"

"I want to be big and strong like you," I replied.

Many of the men howled with laughter. Even the manager struggled to keep a straight face. He walked me over to the desk by the entrance. A rack full of glossy magazines and shelves of different-sized jars and canisters filled the small lobby. The jars were filled with protein powder and supplements.

"How old are you, kid?" he asked.

"I'm eight years old," I said in a grown-up, strong voice.

"Listen, kid," he said. "You're too young to be lifting weights. Your bones have a lot of growing to do. When you start high school, come back and see me." He pointed at the magazines and asked, "Which magazine do you like the most?"

I pointed to a magazine with a giant, muscle-bound man on the cover.

He took it off the shelf and said, "Here, kid, you can have it for free." I cherished that magazine. I put it on my dresser at home and looked at it every day.

A few years later, I noticed how skinny I was compared to the other upper classmates in high school, so I went back to Joe Weider's gym. I asked the manager what I needed to do to add muscle. He sold me a plastic container of protein powder. He told me to start lifting weights and to take the powder. The powder was the worst thing I'd ever tasted in my life. I mixed it with water, but it never seemed to blend completely. Still, I choked it down.

I kept lifting weights and drinking the protein powder. When I started, I was six feet tall and 110 pounds. When I graduated from high school, I was six feet two inches and 195 pounds. Somewhere during that transition, my father hit me, and he could tell it didn't faze me anymore.

I stood there looking at him as if to say, *Is that all you got?* I could feel I had a crazy look in my eyes, and I knew that if he hit me again, I would knock him on his ass. I'm not sure if he was afraid of me for my size or if he remembered the day he knocked out his own father. I think it was a little of both. From that day forward, he never hit me again. My three older siblings had all moved on and were out of the house. That meant I was the oldest child living in the house. When I was home, my father never raised a hand to my mother or younger sister and brother. If I was not in the house, he still abused them.

By the time I graduated from high school in 1977, I estimate I'd been in six hundred fights. The majority of those fights were in the streets with no adults around. When I was young, no one ever got hurt badly, but as a child, I didn't know that. All I knew was that there were a lot of people gathered around, and they wanted to see someone get hurt.

When I got older, things changed. People did get hurt. Friends would have to go to the hospital. I went to the hospital. I punched a guy so hard one time, my pinkie and ring finger knuckles were pushed back about an inch, and I could see the bones and ligaments in my hand. It took nine stitches to close the wound. My cousin was shot through the heart and died within minutes. I had friends who were either murdered or committed suicide. The schoolyard fights had escalated to a point where the violence was out of control.

Recommendation:

From this, I draw two conclusions. One, people who physically abuse their families are cowards. Two, as a child in an abusive home, I was a victim. Once I got old enough and big enough, I chose not to volunteer to be a victim. On more than one occasion, my dad would revert to his old habit. All I had to do was get near him, and he would withdraw—sometimes, just in time. He would have his hand drawn back against my mom or a sibling, and when I entered the room, he would immediately get control of himself. Often, he would leave the house at that point, angry and embarrassed.

When Jesus came into my heart, and I could feel the presence of the Holy Spirit in my life, I wrote my dad a long letter to tell him I loved him and forgave him. Weeks later, we talked over the phone. I could hear my mom in the background telling him to thank me for the letter.

"Oh yeah," he said, "Thank you for the letter you wrote me. It was nice." We never spoke about it again.

> Do not take revenge, my dear friends, but leave room for God's wrath, for it is written: "It is mine to avenge; I will repay," says the Lord. On the contrary: "If your enemy is hungry, feed him; If he is thirsty, give him something to drink. In doing this, you will heap burning coals on his head." Do not be overcome by evil, but overcome evil with good.
>
> Romans 12:19-21

I never raised a hand to my father. I believe God protected me and protected him. I'd survived six hundred street fights. Years of lifting weights and drinking protein drinks had made me big and strong. I could hurt my father badly. In hindsight, I'm glad I never raised a hand to him.

Verbal Abuse Hurts Too

Growing up with the fear of getting kicked or smacked by my parents wasn't easy. On top of that, I lived in a neighborhood where I never knew if I was going to get into a fight. It was stressful to go to school, not knowing if half a hundred students would surround me and yell "Fight, fight, fight!" at the top of their lungs.

I won more fights than I lost. Sometimes, I cried after winning a fight. One of my friends would walk up to me and say, "You won the fight. Why are you crying?"

Still shaking and crying and celebrating, I would reply, "I don't know why I'm crying."

Part of me felt good because I won, and part of me felt bad because I just beat someone up because the crowd surrounded us and demanded that we fight. I didn't beat anyone up because I wanted to. I felt my fist smash into another person's face, and it didn't feel normal. When I was in the fight, it felt like the world moved in slow motion. My hands felt like they weighed twenty pounds each. My brain processed things so quickly; it felt like it was going to blow a fuse. I had to win, or I was going to get my face smashed in. The worst was when I got a black eye because the other kids would tease me about it for a week.

Even with all the stress and worry and fear and physical pain, plus the humility of getting my butt kicked, nothing compared to how degraded I felt after my dad's verbal attacks.

The slightest thing could set him off. Some of the things I knew. For example, if I dropped something that made a loud noise and startled him, I became his target. He had a near-perfect hit rate when he set his eyes on a target. Other times, I had no idea I was going to set him off. Maybe I told one of my siblings a joke, and we laughed too loud. Other times, something that had set him off in the past would not set him off in the present. So, I was on a stress roller coaster. It was a constant drain, physically and mentally, not knowing what would cause him to explode into anger and violence.

You can't change how people treat you or what they say about you. All you can change is how you react to it.

My dad's verbal abuse cut deeply into my soul. He would scream insults two inches from my face like an army drill sergeant. If I hadn't been slapped already, a sure way to get slapped was to say something. I would just stand there as still as possible and not say anything, hoping it would end.

He would scream, "I hate you; I wish you were never born! I wish you were dead!"

Words no child should ever hear.

As a young child, I couldn't understand how my father could wish I'd never been born. I searched my young mind for an answer to the question. I still can't understand it today. I have four children, and I can't imagine ever feeling that way.

At times, I felt guilty when my dad was going after one of my siblings because I was relieved that he'd targeted them instead of me. At first, I tried as hard as I could to get away from the scene. If I could escape, I'd run to the part of the house that was the farthest away from him. If I could, I'd run outside. Once I felt safe, the guilt began. I'd struggle with that and think, *Am I bad for being glad it wasn't me?*

I had to listen to my father degrade me, my mother, my three brothers, and my two sisters for years. I was physically and mentally exhausted. I left for Georgia Tech at age eighteen, and I never lived at home again.

Recommendation:

Reading the New Testament has contributed a lot to my healing over the years. I've read a lot of self-help books. I still believe the New Testament is the best manual for living a great life. I try to read the Bible every day. I say *try* because I do occasionally miss a day.

> (Jesus said) "I have told you these things, so that in me you may have peace. In this world you will have trouble. But take heart! I have overcome the world."
>
> John 16:33

Nellie, my therapist for four years, helped me work through my physical and verbal abuse issues. Nellie taught me that as a child, I was a victim. I was not responsible for the abuse with which my parents ruled the home. They chose to be that way because they had their own issues. Still, it took years before I began to believe it wasn't my fault.

The other thing Nellie taught me was that we're responsible for how we react to what other people say. I'm still working on this one. When I was a kid, if you wanted to get someone to fight, all you had to do was say something horrible about his mother in front of other kids. It worked every time. The concept holds true today. Taking responsibility for how you react to other people's words is hard work. You can't change how people treat you or what they say about you. All you can change is how you react to it.

Sexual Abuse

I don't have firsthand knowledge of sexual abuse, but many people close to me have been sexually abused. Their stories break my heart.

I dated a woman for four years who I'll call Beth. About six months into our relationship, I woke up one Saturday morning, and Beth was gone. Well, at least she wasn't in bed with me, which was the last place I'd seen her. It would have been unusual for her to leave without saying goodbye. I didn't panic. I got up and made my way through the house. She wasn't there. I started to panic. I threw on some clothes and headed outside. As I went through the door, I saw Beth sitting on the porch steps, her arms holding her knees tight against her chest so that she was all curled up in a ball. She had her head down and was crying.

I sat down next to her and put my arm around her.

"What's up, babe? Why are you crying? You're scaring me," I said. My mind churned. I had no idea what was going on. She didn't look up, and she didn't answer me.

She let me pull her close and wrap both of my arms around her. She melted into my body. Still crying, Beth wouldn't look at me. I held her for a few minutes and didn't say anything.

Beth resisted a little, but she let me put my fingers under her chin and slowly lift her face. Our eyes locked, and I could see the pain and vulnerability in her eyes.

Speaking softly, I asked, "What is bothering you?"

She put her head down again and said in a quiet voice, "I'm afraid to tell you."

I could feel my heart rate increasing. I couldn't imagine what was coming next. Growing up in a household where I did not trust anything to be what it seemed, I thought she was going to break up with me. Maybe she'd slept with someone else. But I wanted to give Beth the benefit of the doubt, and I didn't want to judge her based on some vague suspicion. I held her close for several more minutes.

Beth started to open up to me. "I'm scared to tell why I'm crying."

"Babe, please don't be afraid."

"I feel like if I tell you, you'll reject me."

"You need to trust me."

Beth cried for a few more minutes. I didn't want to push her, and at this point, I didn't care if she told me why she was crying. I just wanted her to stop crying and be all right.

"When I was a young girl, my mom got divorced. She eventually met someone else. One thing led to another, and she remarried. My stepfather sexually abused me."

I had a million questions. My first thought was to find this guy and beat him half to death. My heart raced, and it took all I had to stay calm.

"How old were you?" I asked.

"Eight or nine."

I couldn't hold back. "This guy had sex with you when you were eight years old?" I asked in horror.

"No," Beth said without hesitation.

I didn't know what to say.

"He did things to me," Beth said.

"Like what?" I asked, confused.

"He would perform oral sex on me."

My head exploded. For an instant, I understood how a human could kill another human. I jumped up and started pacing.

Beth said, "I was afraid you'd react like this. Are you upset with me?"

"Are you kidding? I want to kill this guy right now. Do you know where he is?"

"No."

"What's his name?"

"No, you can't look for him. I'm not going to tell you his name."

"Baby, I love you. None of this is your fault. I'm sorry I'm so upset. I'm angry that you had to deal with that. I'm not upset with you."

It did impact our relationship, though, because after she told me, I was afraid I would traumatize Beth, and Beth was afraid I thought less of her. At first, there were some awkward moments. As time passed, it became less and less of an issue, and we got to a place where we both felt comfortable in our relationship.

I put up with physical and verbal abuse, and it was terrifying. When my male and female friends share their sexual abuse stories with me, it's incomprehensible.

Recommendation:

> Jesus said, "Father forgive them for they do not know what they are doing."
>
> Luke 23:34

In this passage, Jesus was talking about the centurions who beat and tortured him and were about to crucify him. It wasn't easy for me to forgive my father. But when I did, it lifted a burden off my shoulders. For years, I dragged around a large bag of stones that weighed me down and wore me out. When I truly in my heart forgave my father, it was as if Jesus came to stand beside me and said, "You can let go of the bag of rocks now."

Forgiveness is freeing. I struggled with understanding how God could forgive me. It wasn't until I learned to forgive people that I understood God could forgive me because he loves me so much.

Nellie also taught me that when I was a child, I was a victim with no way to escape, but that adults who allow themselves to be abused are volunteers, not victims. If you're in an abusive environment, don't stay there. Get away. Don't be a volunteer.

Finally, get help. When I was young, I couldn't understand why my mom stayed with my dad. I remember thinking to myself, *You are the adult here. You are our mother. Get us out of here.* Looking back, there was nowhere my mom could turn for help. Today there are organizations that can help. They start by taking a mother and her children away from the abusive situation. My first recommendation is to turn to God, pray, and read the Bible. Second, reach out to people you can trust and ask for their advice. Third, search the internet for organizations that offer assistance and contact them.

Remember, as a child, you are a victim. As an adult, you are a volunteer.

5

LIVE WITH YOURSELF—YOU DON'T HAVE A CHOICE

I grew up in a rough neighborhood, which meant that I knew high school was going to be rough. I entered high school just as the World Trade Center Twin Towers were being built. For four years, as I walked to school, I saw the towers going up, floor by floor. I couldn't believe how tall they were when completed.

High school is hard. As a teenager, it was difficult for me to figure things out. Ralph Waldo Emerson High School was contained in a single building with about 1,400 students. The building took up every inch of the land it sat on. The edge of the building went right to the sidewalk. No grass. No trees. It was three stories tall with a full basement. The basement served as the makeshift gym, and the ground floor, second, and third floor

High school is hard. As a teenager, it was difficult for me to figure things out.

held classrooms. Except for the basement, the entire building was U-shaped, with classrooms on both sides of a central hall. The walls were lined with lockers. Between class, the halls filled to capacity. There were so many students, I could hardly walk down the hall. There were four major stairwells. The stairs were about eight feet wide, which allowed a lot of people to be bustling up and down. We didn't have a proper gym, swimming pool, field, or stadium—just a big concrete and wood building.

I was fourteen when I entered Emerson in September 1973. The amount of crap going through my head was crazy. *When should I get a girlfriend? How do I get a girlfriend? How do I get in with the cool kids? Am I blow-drying my hair the right way? Do I have nice enough clothes? Will I make the football team? Will I start? Am I smart enough to pass my classes? Will anyone find out I am poor? Will anyone find out my dad is abusive? Will anyone find out I smoke pot?* The voice in my head was endless, and it exhausted me.

I soon had most of my answers. I made friends. I made the football team, and I ran on the track team. I found a girlfriend. I was the yearbook sports photographer. I went to Boys' State, where we spent four days on a college campus modeling how the New Jersey State government operated. Academically, I graduated number nine out of 310 graduates. Through all of this, I drank too much, and I sold marijuana in the hallways.

High school is hard for everyone. As a teenager, it was difficult for me to figure things out. Many of the people I knew had difficulties as well. I would say my neighborhood was lower- to middle-class because a lot of blue-collar people live in Union City, but I don't believe it matters what your social ranking is when you're trying to make friends and find out where you fit in a high school environment. I was lucky that

I played football and track and was involved in other school activities. I also learned that I was a very good student, and I knew that was going to be my ticket out of Union City.

My oldest son Andrew graduated from high school in May of 2011. At the time, I was on a short-term assignment (two years) working as the head of Strategy and Process Execution in the Risk Management Department at Barclays Bank. Since it was only two years, my family didn't go to London with me, but I got Andrew an internship at Barclays Bank Global Headquarters, and he spent the summer after graduation in Barclays' Anti-Money Laundering (AML) department. We lived together in Canary Wharf and walked a few blocks to work each day.

At the end of the summer, I asked, "Working in London for the summer at Barclays Bank was a huge opportunity for you. What did you learn?"

Andrew took the question seriously, and he thought about it for a few minutes. He broke the silence, "Dad, I learned two things."

In my mind, I thought, *Only two things! You must have learned a hundred things.* Being patient, I asked, "What were they?"

"First, I learned I don't want a desk job. Second, the cool kids in high school are not the type of people I see at the executive level."

These two lessons were simple yet life-changing. He'd been exposed to senior leaders and had figured out the cool kids never hold a senior position at a global bank. I could see him taking a more serious look at adulthood after his internship.

Andrew loved being outside, and he loved playing sports, like me. I sat at a desk all day but never considered whether I liked having a desk job. Making the decision, at eighteen years old, that he didn't want to be inside behind a desk all day was life-changing.

Recommendation:

Learn to live with yourself. It can be hard to love yourself. Loving yourself is a lifelong journey. God loves you completely. Don't use drugs or alcohol or food or sex or whatever to cope with life. Know that God created you, and you are awesome just the way you are.

My mother and other adults often told me, "Life is short. It goes by fast."

I never knew what to do with that information. At eighteen, most people don't understand what it means.

For just one moment, try to imagine you are fifty-eight versus eighteen. To demonstrate my idea, add fifty-eight years to the year you were born. For example, if you were born in 2000, imagine it is 2058. I promise you, when you are fifty-eight, you'll be thinking, *Life is short. It goes by fast.* You are never too young to start thinking about what you want out of life. Dream. Take responsibility. Plan and live a fulfilling, God-centered life right now, no matter how old you are.

Live every day to its fullest.

The Real World

My parents couldn't afford to pay for me to go to college. So, for me, the real world hit when I was eighteen. I was off to Georgia Tech, not sure how I was going to make it. I had saved all my life for college, but after a few months, it became apparent that I didn't have enough saved up to cover the costs.

To stay sane, I exercised and ran several miles every day. I'd run track in high school but never thought I was good enough to run in college. Still, I felt a strong desire to run, so I walked into the head track coach's office and said, "I'd like to try out for the track team."

Buddy Fowlkes asked in a thick Southern drawl, "Son, what events did you run, and what were your personal bests?"

"I ran the 120-yard high hurdles in 14.9 and the 330-yard intermediate hurdles in 39.8."

Coach Fowlkes said, "I can't promise you anything, but you're welcome to work out with us for a few days."

I made the Georgia Tech Men's Varsity Track Team. I thought I had died and gone to heaven. When I got my competition uniform, I was elated. It was made of the finest material, and I remember trying it on in my dorm room. The tank top was white, and the shorts were gold. The sweat jacket and pants were made of a shiny gold material. Sewn on the back of the sweat jacket in big letters was *Georgia Tech Track.* I got new running shoes, new sprinting shoes, a travel bag, and a special gold garment bag to carry my sweats in. It was one of the best days of my life.

I carried a full load of classes. I was in a fraternity, but I lived with my girlfriend. I was on the track team, and I worked twenty hours per week. Many days I had less than two dollars in my pocket. Being on my own was a lot harder than I thought it would be.

Being a young adult is difficult. The responsibilities thrust upon you can be crushing. Persevere.

One of my favorite jobs was working at a custom-made bedspread factory in the late 1970s. One day, we received a package of royal-blue silk from China. Robert, the owner, hand-carried the material out into the factory, something he'd never done before. As he walked toward me, package in hand, he said, "Bruce, I have silk in my hand that's from China, and it cost over $1,000." In 1979, a $1,000 wholesale price for the fabric was a ridiculous amount of money.

Robert very carefully opened the package. The royal-blue color mesmerized me. Even more impressive was the texture. The fabric floated through my fingers and was the softest, smoothest fabric I had ever touched.

Robert snapped me out of my love affair with the fabric. He raised his voice and said, "Please do not get it hung up on the nails!"

On the factory floor, we had three twelve-foot-wide sewing machines. I didn't have enough experience to operate the sewing machines. To sew a bedspread, we attached the material to large twelve-foot square frames. Around the edge of the frame were strips of wood with sharp nails, like tack strips that hold carpet in place in homes.

The cliché "time is money" applied here. When I was a new employee, I couldn't believe how fast the experienced employees could frame a bedspread. As I learned and tried to go faster, I often stabbed one of my fingers with a nail. Bleeding all over the place while handling expensive fabric was not good. For the first month or so, I had Band-Aids on at least three fingers. If I was in a hurry and wasn't careful, I could catch the bedspread material on these nails as I lifted it into the middle of the frame. If I damaged the material near the edge, it was okay, but if I damaged the material in the middle of the bedspread, it was a disaster. Robert and his son Herschel would then come out of their office onto the shop floor and inspect the damage. If it was bad, they had to order new material and inform the customer of the delay, and I'd get the stink eye for a good day or two.

Robert was crystal clear when he told me not to snag the silk on the nails. I framed the silk without damaging it. I knew it was a big deal when Herschel came out of the front office to sew the silk bedspread himself. Herschel was the best sewing machine operator in the company. The finished product was amazing, and I got to pack it for shipment. Since no one was around, I closed my eyes and swished my hand slowly back and forth over the silk for several minutes before closing up the box.

Recommendation:

Always dream. Look out ahead two to three years and always be dreaming about what you want your life to look like. My dreams included being a pastry chef in Manhattan, a pediatrician, a spy plane pilot, and an engineer. Today, my dream is to help young adults navigate the first decade of adulthood, helping them plan and live a God-centered, fulfilling life.

Being a young adult is difficult. The responsibilities thrust upon you can be crushing. Persevere. Be yourself; everyone else is taken.

> Let your eyes look straight ahead;
> Fix your gaze directly before you.
> Give careful thought to the paths for your feet
> And be steadfast in your ways.
>
> Proverbs 4:25-26

Are You Mature Yet?

I persevered and graduated with a Bachelor of Science in Industrial Engineering, and at twenty-two years old, I was on my own as a professional in Miami, Florida. On my first day of work, I met Daniel. He had served several years in the military and was a few years older than the typical college graduate. He was a nice guy, and we hit it off. It didn't take long for us to realize we were both broke and needed a place to stay. I found an apartment in Coconut Grove and approached Dan.

"Do you want to stay with me and share the expenses until we both get on our feet?"

Dan replied, "Absolutely!"

I came from a college setting where I lived with roommates all the time. Dan was accustomed to living with roommates from being in the military. It made it easy for us to get along.

Neither of us had much. I ordered rental furniture. The only thing I purchased was a small TV from Sears, opening a line of credit with the company in the process. This was the second time I went into debt. The first time was for college loans.

"So, how are we going to do the sleeping arrangements?" Dan asked.

"I suggest we flip a coin, and whoever wins gets the bed for the first month, and then we switch each month after that."

Dan agreed. I won the toss and got the bed for the first month; Dan slept on the sofa. There was another issue.

I asked, "What if one of us picks up a girl, and we bring her back to the apartment, and it's our month to sleep on the sofa?"

"If one of us is bringing home a girl," Dan said, "we get the bedroom, no questions asked."

"Done!" I said.

Dan told me that because of his military training, he had an unusual issue. "Don't ever wake me up if I'm sleeping," he cautioned, "because I will attack you."

"You're messing with me," I chuckled.

"No, I'm serious," Dan replied.

One night, after spending time with some friends in Coconut Grove, I came back to the apartment. My lips were chapped, and my Chapstick was in the bedroom where Dan was sound asleep. I fretted for thirty minutes. Should I go in there or not? I finally decided I could be super quiet and not wake him.

I turned off all the lights in the apartment and slowly opened the bedroom door. I walked past the foot of the bed as quietly as I could. I gently picked up my Chapstick from the dresser and turned to leave the room. I took one step, and Dan came flying off the bed and pounced on me. He bear-hugged me, and we both went flying into the dresser.

"Dan, wake up! Dan, wake up! It's me, Bruce! Wake up!" I shouted the whole time.

We were both big guys. I was six feet two inches tall and 220 pounds. Dan was six feet four inches tall and 240 pounds. We were both in good shape, and we both knew how to fight. I was trying to break away and defend myself. We tossed each other around, then fell into the closet, hangers and clothes flying everywhere in the dark. I got Dan to stop fighting, but he still wouldn't let go of me. I tried to stay calm until he fully woke up.

"Oh my God. Are you okay? I'm so sorry," Dan kept repeating. Eventually, we started laughing. We laughed so hard neither of us could talk. I never woke him up again.

Dan explained that his military training and some of the missions he was on caused him to develop a keen sense of his surroundings, even when he was asleep. If you got near him while he was asleep, he perceived it as a threat, and it meant life or death to him. I'm so glad he had warned me. It allowed me to stay calm and keep calling out to him to wake up. No one was hurt, but it was crazy in the moment.

We shared the expense of our one-bedroom apartment in order to gain financial stability. Dan moved out after a few months, and I stayed. At first, I was thrilled to have my own apartment. After a few months, it got lonely. I craved fellowship and love. Being alone was hard to cope with. I didn't have any close friends in Miami, and the loneliness was more profound on weekends. Coconut Grove was one of the most hustling and bustling places in Miami, and I loved walking through the marketplace full of people, but I still felt alone.

Recommendation:

Whether or not you are ready, you have to grow up, be mature, and take care of yourself. You will run into difficulties, but that's how you learn and grow.

Make friends with like-minded people. You only need a few close friends.

Get involved in your community. Join a church, synagogue, or mosque. Volunteer. I am part of a church, and I serve there in many ways. Every time I serve, I get more out than I put in. Join a club. I am on the board of directors for Urban K-Life in Saint Louis, where I help inner-city high-school students graduate and go to college. The rewards are amazing.

6

HAVE YOU EVER HIT ROCK BOTTOM?

The parking lot to my North Miami condo was just off a five-lane major road that had two lanes in each direction and a turn lane in the middle. To pull into the building, you drove over the sidewalk and right into the parking lot. The building, which had thirteen units, was at the end of the parking lot. The lot was a near-perfect rectangle. Sitting back on the lot, the building was secluded and, for the most part, quiet. It was a nice building. I lived on the second floor. The walkway was open-air.

South Florida is almost intolerably hot in the summer and tolerable for the rest of the year. I lived ten minutes from the beach, and my best friend, Don, lived around the block, an easy walk. It seemed that life was good, but while I was living in this condo, my life took a nosedive.

As the cliché goes, I hit rock bottom. My marriage was falling apart, and I was ruining my life with alcohol and cocaine. While I was still legally married, I started seeing a married woman who I'll call Joy. When my wife discovered what was going on, she got so angry she punched me in the face.

When Joy's husband, Al, discovered our affair, he came to my office. I showed him into my office and hoped he wouldn't make a scene. Al looked like he had stayed up all night and was visibly shaken. He was livid. I was ashamed.

I hit rock bottom. My marriage was falling apart, and I was ruining my life with alcohol and cocaine.

Even though I didn't know him, Al said, "How could you do this to me?"

"I'm sorry," I told him, and meant it. I was sorry he was hurting.

He asked, "Will you stop seeing her?"

I wondered if I should lie or tell him the truth. I went for the truth. I said, "I can't promise that I'll stop seeing her."

Al lifted himself two or three inches out of his seat, his face animated like some crazy cartoon character. "What?" he screamed. "Are you kidding me?"

I thought he was going to come across my desk and punch me in the face. I felt like such an idiot and didn't know how to respond.

Al said, "In the Old Testament, you and Joy would have been taken outside the village and stoned to death." As he left my office, he mumbled, "You are such an asshole."

How much more could I mess up my life? About the only thing going well was my job. Yet, at times I went into work so hung over I'm sure my coworkers could smell alcohol oozing out of my pores. It took all I had to function and make it through the workday.

Life is a series of choices. Making bad choices has its consequences. I made my own bad choices. No one else made them for me. I still make bad choices. I believe the devil is in his happy place when I make poor decisions and my life is a mess.

Recommendation:

At the base of our brains is the amygdala. The study of emotional intelligence tells us that the amygdala is the first stop in our brain when we respond to our environment. If you give yourself a fraction of a second, your brain can process your emotional response through your rear lobe and then your frontal lobe and process a complete rational thought.

However, we sometimes override the natural process and react right after the amygdala is done processing and isn't letting us complete the rational thought. I'm not a brain scientist, but I believe I was making snap decisions and not letting my brain process them. Alcohol, drugs, and highly charged emotional events all contribute to making snap decisions. It has cost me dearly. Give your brain that extra fraction of a second, or even two or three seconds, to make rational decisions.

Break Bad Habits

Making changes takes discipline and fortitude. Research has shown that it takes twenty-one days of intentionally changing a behavior for the change to even have a chance to remain in place. How many times have you committed to going to the gym or running, playing tennis, swimming, bike riding, and so forth, only to quit after a week or two? It's hard to change. The examples of things people want to change are numerous: lose weight, stop smoking, stop drinking, stop driving aggressively, stop using drugs, and stop procrastinating about breaking bad habits. You have to reach deep inside yourself to find the willpower to change. Asking God to help you can make all the difference in your success.

In his book, *The Power of Habit: Why We Do What We Do in Life and Business*, Charles Duhigg presents his concept, "The Habit Loop."

> This process within our brain is a three-step loop. First there is a *cue*, a trigger that tells your brain to go into automatic mode and which habit to use. Then there is the *routine*, which can be physical or mental or emotional. Finally, there is a *reward*, which helps your brain figure out if this particular loop is worth remembering for the future.
>
> Over time, this loop—cue, routine, reward; cue, routine, reward—becomes more and more automatic. The cue and reward become intertwined until a powerful sense of anticipation and craving emerges. Eventually, whether in a chilly MIT laboratory or your driveway, a habit is born.

When I quit smoking, this habit loop became apparent to me. I didn't want people at work to know I smoked, so I tried to hide it. Whenever I got into my car alone, I reached for the glove box, popped it open, and grabbed the pack of cigarettes.

For months after I quit, when my mind raced and I juggled five thoughts at once, I would get in my car and pop open the glove box. There were other triggers, too: waking up in the morning, drinking the first cup of coffee, finishing a meal, having a couple of drinks, and just before going to bed, to name a few. For a few months, I even went so far as to reach for the pack of cigarettes, but I no longer kept a pack of cigarettes there. I would chuckle inside and think to myself, *I can't believe I just reached for the cigarettes.*

Duhigg proposes that once we program a habit into our brain's computer, we can never erase it. To me, that was the most disturbing part of the book. I created my bad habits. No one followed me around with a gun to my head and made me create them.

Duhigg's Golden Rule of Habit Change is, "You can't extinguish a bad habit; you can only change it."

It was the light at the end of the tunnel for me. I was depressed that every bad habit I ever created would be saved in my brain. However, although I might not be able to erase the habit, I could change it. Duhigg proposes:

HOW IT WORKS.
USE THE SAME CUE.
PROVIDE THE SAME REWARD.
CHANGE THE ROUTINE.

When I reached for the glove box, I wanted a cigarette. The new routine I taught myself was to repeat over and over in my mind, *Healthy lungs, clean lungs, healthy body, healthy lungs, clean lungs, healthy body…* It worked.

Don't create bad habits. Let your "no" mean no.

Choose Your Friends Carefully

One habit that's difficult to change is how we choose our friends. It can be detrimental when we constantly choose the wrong friends. I have found there will *always* be people willing to party. They wanted to party, and they encouraged me to party.

Have you ever known someone whose friends weren't good for them? You watch from afar and shake your head in disbelief as they continue to be attracted to the same kind of people. Over and over, they choose friends who hurt them.

Just as I was responsible for creating bad habits, I was also responsible for choosing friends who weren't good for me.

Recommendation:

One of the things I learned in Alcoholics Anonymous was to put my friends into two categories. Category One was those who would help me in my quest to be sober, and Category Two was those who would hurt me in my quest to be sober. I was amazed how many would hurt me in my quest. But still, 100 percent of the responsibility for remaining sober was on me, not my friends. If they wanted to keep their lifestyle, I had no business judging them. It was my responsibility to remain sober.

Be intentional about the friends you choose.

7

ADDICTION IS A PROBLEM

Sara M. Gilmore Elementary School sat in the middle of a square city block. The school property ran through the middle of the block from Sixteenth Street in the front to Fifteenth Street in the back. I drank my first quart of beer in 1971, in the dark, on the doorstep of my elementary school. I was twelve years old.

At night, older people, eighteen to twenty-five years old, hung out at the back entrance to the large schoolyard. They were scary to me. They smoked cigarettes and pot and drank beer, wine, and hard liquor from bottles in brown paper bags. I'm pretty sure they took other drugs too. There was one guy who was so big and tough that no one messed with him.

José had dark, overgrown hair and an overgrown beard to go with it. He even looked crazy. He was thick and heavyset, like he could run through a brick wall. A quart of beer was thirty-five cents, and the legal drinking age was eighteen. I had heard that if you paid José, he would buy you beer. One evening, I worked up the courage to approach him. As I crept toward him, he noticed me coming. He let me keep coming.

Suddenly he said in a loud voice, "What do you want?" I thought I was going to die right there on the spot.

I squeaked out, "Can you buy me beer?"

José leaned in closer to me, and this time, he spoke in a much softer voice. He said, "A quart of beer is thirty-five cents. If you give me fifty cents and wait right here, I'll bring you a quart of beer."

In my mind, I thought this was a big rip-off. But if I wanted beer, I had to pay up. I gave José fifty cents and waited. I stood there waiting in a group of adults. I was skinny. I was afraid. They were a rough bunch. After what seemed like forever, José returned with my quart of beer in a brown paper bag and handed it to me.

I took the beer and hurriedly walked through the large school yard and up fifteen concrete stairs to one of the smaller schoolyards. It was dark. I was scared. I couldn't believe how big and heavy the quart of beer felt. The thoughts running through my mind were, *Can drinking a quart of beer kill me? What if my dad finds out? Would the police come through the dark schoolyard?* I sat there, drank the entire quart of beer, and left the bottle on the doorstep.

I went out of the front of the schoolyard, so I didn't have to pass José and his friends. I headed toward Summit Avenue, a main street. It was well lit with tall, bright streetlights. Summit Avenue was wide and had ten-foot-wide concrete sidewalks on both sides. There were storefronts at the street level with houses and apartments built on top of the businesses. Some of the apartment buildings were six stories high. There was always traffic on Summit Avenue.

Here I was, a small, twelve-year-old boy—maybe seventy-five pounds—walking down Summit Avenue after drinking a quart of Miller High Life, a smile plastered on my face. The streetlights and headlights didn't look like they usually did—they looked like stars. My balance was slightly off as I lumbered down the street. I didn't have a plan where I was going; I just knew I wasn't going home. I wasn't worried anymore. Fear was no longer in the forefront of my mind. It felt euphoric to not care. I thought, *I have to do this again.*

Having José as my beer runner literally saved my life. José bought me beer whenever I wanted it for over a year. One night, I was sitting on the wooden steps of a temporary trailer classroom in the Gilmore School schoolyard, and I overheard a conversation. José and a skinny, nervous guy were plotting to rob a local merchant.

I'll call the skinny guy Doug. Doug always played stickball in the schoolyard and was a cheater and a hothead. José and Doug had learned that every night the merchant walked home with the proceeds of the day in a brown paper bag. They were going to rob him. When I heard the conversation, I wanted to run, but I was afraid to draw attention to myself. But Doug noticed me on the steps.

He started to pace and fling his arms in all directions and told José, "We need to kill this kid. He heard our conversation."

José told him, "No way are we going to kill this kid." Looking at me, he said, "Are you going to tell anyone about our conversation?"

"No, absolutely not!" I said. I'd grown up in the streets, and there was a code. Never snitch on anyone. José could tell I meant what I said.

About a month later, word got around that the merchant had been robbed by two men. The merchant had refused to give up the bag of money. One of the robbers hit him in the head with a metal pipe, and they took the bag of money. The merchant was in the hospital for a few days. If I hadn't developed a relationship with José, I could have been killed.

Recommendation:

It was a bad choice to start using alcohol to ease my pain and anxiety at age twelve. I've read research that states that the earlier someone starts using drugs and alcohol, the higher the probability it will cause serious problems later in life. In my case, the research was true. I learned early how to numb myself. As I got older, I wanted more. I would drink too much alcohol, smoke too much pot, or use too much cocaine. I graduated to smoking pot around sixteen years old and cocaine at twenty-two. Once I took the first drink or drug, I couldn't stop.

If you are addicted, get help. The number of resources where you can find help is overwhelming. If you haven't started using alcohol or drugs, don't start. You heard me right. I recommend you *never* use illegal drugs or drink alcohol.

Illegal for a Reason

The Southern Division of Florida Power and Light (FPL) encompassed all of Metro Dade County, which covered all of metro Miami. It was the most densely populated division of the five FPL divisions. The Southern Division headquarters was housed in a large, four-story rectangular building. The exterior was not all that impressive, but the interior had a high-end design with upscale furnishings.

Angel and I started working at the Southern Division headquarters on the same day, January 4, 1982. We were both hired into the FPL Energy Conversation department with nine other recently-graduated engineers. He was an engineer from the University of Miami and was a native of Miami. Angel was a quiet, good-looking Cuban. He was well built and carried himself in a way that made me think I wouldn't want to get into a fight with him.

After about three weeks, we arrived in the parking lot at the same time. I pulled up in the cheapest version of a station wagon with the FPL logo on the door, my loaner from the company because I didn't own a car. Angel pulled up in a white, convertible Porsche Targa.

I broke the ice. "Good morning," I said.

"Good morning."

I asked a dumb question, partly in disbelief and partly because I was intimidated. "Is that your car?"

"Yes, it is," replied Angel.

He was pretty calm and handled my question with grace. We chatted about his car as we walked across the large parking lot and up the stairs into the building. It was the beginning of a great friendship.

We soon bonded, and before long, we started doing things together outside of work. One day, we left the office and went to lunch at a Cuban restaurant called Latin America.

On the way back to the office, Angel asked, "Do you mind if we swing by the bank?"

Did I mind being seen in a Porsche Targa with the top down, driving around with Angel? Dumb question.

"Of course, we can swing by the bank," I replied. I was actually thinking, *Can we drive around Miami all afternoon, so I can meet my future wife?*

We went through the bank drive-through lane closest to the building. As we rolled up to the window, Angel asked me, "Hey, can you open the glove box and give me the cash in there?"

Oblivious, taking in the gorgeous South Florida day, I popped open the glove box. The door swung down and right in front of my eyes was a three-inch-thick stack of cash with a large silver revolver sitting on top of it. I was dumbfounded and sat there staring at the money and the gun.

With a little more sense of urgency, Angel asked, "Hey, can you give me the cash?"

"Uh…I…uh…there's a gun on top of it," I said softly because I didn't want to say the word "gun" too loudly at a bank drive-up window.

"Move the gun," Angel snapped back.

Replying quietly, I said, "I don't know how. I've never touched a gun before."

"Just pick it up and move it. But don't point it at me."

With my right hand, I gently picked up the gun by the grip, making sure my fingers didn't go anywhere near the trigger. I grabbed the stack of cash with my left hand and passed it to Angel. I kept holding the gun, making sure it was pointed down and not at him. There were a lot of $100 bills, thousands of dollars in cash. I thought, *That is a lot of money. How can he get away with depositing that much cash?*

Angel handed the cash to an attractive woman inside the teller window. He flirted with the teller and spoke to her in Spanish. She flirted back. I didn't know what they were saying, but I could tell they knew each other.

We deposited the cash and drove away from the bank. After a brief awkward silence, I asked, "What was that?"

Angel said, "It was just some cash I made from working over the weekend."

I left it alone. I knew what Angel's answer meant and didn't ask another question. I think it was a test to see how I would react, and time would show that I passed the test. Angel trusted me completely.

Back at the office, Angel asked me if I wanted to do cocaine.

A little bit in shock, I said, "No. I've never done it before, and I don't want to try it at work for the first time."

Angel laughed at me. Over the course of the next couple of weeks, Angel would tease me about being afraid to try cocaine.

One Friday afternoon, he said, "Hey, look, we can wait until about four o'clock, and you can try a little pop. I promise you that you will be able to make it until five o'clock, and I'll keep an eye on you."

Around four o'clock, we headed to the men's bathroom. Angel pulled a glossy, aquamarine plastic pod from his pocket. It looked like a smooth rounded rock you might find in a riverbed. The pod was smaller than a ping pong ball. When I first saw it, it looked solid. To my surprise, it had a built-in small spoon. Angel removed the spoon, opened another compartment, stuck the spoon into the belly of the pod, and pulled it out filled with white powder. He snorted it up his nose.

He filled the spoon again and said, "Here, it's your turn." I braced myself and snorted the white powder.

My body knew that whatever I'd just snorted up my nose did not belong there. My self-preservation system kicked in, and my body sent signals to my brain, shouting, *What are you doing?* I regained my composure. Within seconds, I could tell a chemical reaction had taken place in my body. I felt all my senses heighten and my heartbeat increase. Anxiety and fear gripped me, and my adrenaline surged. It felt like a rocket was lifting off inside my body.

Angel asked, "Are you okay?"

"Yes, but wow, that was crazy. Now what do we do?"

"We go back to our desks and act normal."

Act normal! I just did cocaine for the first time, and on top of that, I'm at work. How do I act normal? Angel started to walk out of the bathroom. I wanted to stay there and hide, but I didn't want to leave the only person who knew what I was going through, so I followed Angel, quickly checking my face in the mirror to see if there were any traces of the white powder.

If you are addicted and want help, get help. No one can do this for you. ***You*** *must want to stop and seek help. You need to break the habit of hanging out with the wrong people and putting yourself into situations that support your addiction. Many others have gone before you. You can do this.*

We returned to our desks. Angel sat diagonally across from me, and our backs were to each other. On a Friday after four o'clock, most of the team was wandering around, chatting, and making plans for the weekend. Every few minutes, Angel and I turned around and looked at each other, but we'd have to turn back around because we'd start to laugh. I felt euphoric but still in control.

At about the twenty-minute mark, when no one else was around, Angel whispered across the aisle, "Do you want more?"

Giggling like a couple of kids on Christmas morning, we scooted off to the men's room. We both did another pop.

Then I asked Angel, "Can I have more?"

A serious look of concern came over his face. "I need to warn you. If you don't keep yourself in check, this shit will ruin your life. You can't just give in and do more and more."

"Okay," I replied.

It stopped me in my tracks. I thought to myself, *I can never let this take control of me. I need to manage the desire to go crazy with this stuff.* Angel's comments stuck with me. Twenty minutes later, we did another pop. We agreed to meet up later that night at a club.

We went home to our respective places and changed out of our FPL Energy Conservation uniforms. We were given six uniforms when we started—navy-blue pants and a light-blue golf shirt that had a logo printed on the chest. Angel hated the uniform and folded up the edges of the sleeves like a rebel. Angel had to be different.

All respectable Miamians watched the TV show *Miami Vice* from 10:00 p.m. to 11:00 p.m. on Friday nights, so we met up around 11:30 at a nightclub. I felt like a fish out of water. Angel's friends wore clothes that would cost me a month's worth of pay. The bouncers looked at me as if to say, *Are you really walking in here right now?*

As soon as Angel saw me, he pulled me in, and the bouncers backed off. He introduced me to lots of different people who welcomed me and treated me like family. My anxiety melted away. When the check came, I thought, *Holy cow, how am I going to pay for this?* Without hesitation, Rudy dropped down about $2,000 in cash. I was shocked but grateful. I asked him if I needed to pay anything.

He put his arm around me and said, "Don't worry, I got this."

After our friendship was strong and I felt like Angel trusted me, I asked, "Is there any way I could make money by helping you out with your business?"

Angel was a little surprised but not shocked by my question.

After he thought about it for a few seconds, he replied, "Let me get back to you on that."

I wasn't sure if I would ever hear back, but I was okay with that.

Two weeks later, Angel got me alone and said, "I talked to my people, and here's what we got. Your parents live in New York City, right?"

"Yeah."

"We want you to drive a van with cocaine hidden in it from Miami to New York City. Think of it like you're going on a trip to visit your parents. We'll pay for everything—the van, gas, food, everything. And we'll pay you $2,000 cash."

I was broke, and in 1982, $2,000 could go a long way. In my mind, I'd already spent the money. Then reality set in. *Do I want to do this? I could go to federal prison and ruin my life. But the money would be amazing.*

I asked Angel, "Could I do it only one time?"

Angel pondered my question and replied, "Well, if you did it once, they might ask you to do it again."

"What if I said no?'

Angel paused. "They would kill you."

I briefly contemplated the finality of being killed. I answered, "Well, then, I don't want to do it."

"That's cool. Are we okay?"

I said, "Yeah, I'm okay."

We went about our lives as if I'd never asked the question. Several months passed, and one day, Angel didn't show up at the office. After a couple of days, I tried to call him. He didn't answer my calls. One week, two weeks, and still nothing. Our supervisors had removed his personal stuff from his desk. No one seemed to know what had happened to him. Months later, I found out Angel had been arrested by the United States Drug Enforcement Agency.

As an engineer for FPL, my job took me all over Dade County. If I was within a couple miles of Latin America, the restaurant where Angel and I first went for lunch, I stopped in to eat. My favorite dish was the picadillo. It included sides of white rice, black beans, and soft, fried plantains. The main dish was a bowl filled with ground beef, chopped green olives, raisins, and spices. I would mix the picadillo, black beans, and white rice all together, and I'd eat the whole thing. I saved the soft plantains until the end. They were like dessert.

On this particular day, I was excited to be eating at Latin America. I bounced up the few steps and bounded into the restaurant. It was packed. I glanced around and noticed a few seats open at the counter. I also noticed a man sitting all alone in a booth that would comfortably seat four. After a moment, I realized it was Angel. It had been about a year since I had last seen him.

"Angel!" I shouted his name across the restaurant and sprinted to his booth. As I plopped down, I said, "Angel, holy crap. It's so good to see you."

At the same moment, I noticed four men in suits pop up. A couple of them seemed to be reaching toward their waistbands. Angel made a motion with his hand across his throat as if to signal "cut, false alarm." The four men sat back down but didn't take their eyes off me.

Angel said, "It's good to see you too. I need you to listen to me. I can't talk, but you need to trust me. Get up immediately and go sit at the counter." The look in his eyes told me to do it and not to ask any questions.

"Okay," I replied. I got up and went to an open seat at the counter. My picadillo criollo did not taste as good as it usually did. I was hungry and ate the whole thing, but I felt sick the entire time. When I'd finished lunch, paid my tab, and was leaving, Angel was still sitting in the booth alone. I gave him a half-hearted goodbye wave. He waved back.

I never saw Angel again.

Recommendation:

If you are addicted and want help, get help. No one can do this for you. **You** must want to stop and seek help. You need to break the habit of hanging out with the wrong people and putting yourself into situations that support your addiction. Many others have gone before you. *You can do this.*

I struggled with cocaine for years. When I had to call in sick to work because of my addiction, I wanted to turn my life around. My life started to change when I fell on my knees and asked God to save me. The Holy Spirit of God worked on my heart and my mind to save me. I did not do it alone. My support groups played a major role in my recovery. I saw a psychologist every week. I became active in my church and served others. I attended AA meetings. I read the Bible and prayed. I changed my bad habits.

Tobacco

Don and I were at one of our favorite bars in North Miami, not far from home. He smoked two and a half packs of Newport menthols a day, and I had begged him to quit smoking for years. I told him if he didn't quit smoking, I would start smoking, and he pleaded with me not to start.

This particular evening, we'd had enough drinks that we weren't thinking clearly. The bar was still crowded even though it was getting late.

Don said, "I gotta take a piss."

Urinating was a big production for Don. He would have to raise one arm up in the air and hold onto the wall. He would make all kinds of noises, as if urinating was the best thing in the world. A lot of drama.

"All right, I'll watch your stuff," I replied.

That was another thing about Don; he always had a pile of stuff. The usual pile included keys, one or two packs of Newports, a lighter or matches, his wallet, crumpled-up money, and coins. We could never leave somewhere quickly because he had to pick up and figure out how to carry all his crap.

His cigarettes! I got a cigarette out of the pack and grabbed his lighter. I positioned myself to face the men's room door. I watched and waited. Even with all the smoke, dim lighting, and a bunch of people, I had a clear line of sight to the men's room door. I didn't take my eyes off the door until Don emerged.

He started yelling, "No! No! Don't you dare!" as he hurried to stop me.

He had a big, semi-crowded bar to get through. I stuck the cigarette in my mouth and lit it. I took a big drag and started coughing uncontrollably. *What the hell was that?* I thought. Don finally reached me, and he was pissed off.

"What is wrong with you? Are you a fucking idiot? I am so pissed at you right now."

Don started pacing around like he did when he was upset or nervous. He shook his head and yelled at me. I finally recovered enough to stop coughing.

"Whoa. I think I'm going to pass out," I said. I grabbed onto the bar and slid onto my barstool.

"You're not passing out, you idiot. It's the nicotine giving you a buzz," Don said.

"Holy shit. What a rush. I love it."

I went from thinking I was dying to enjoying a high like none I had experienced before. When I started to smoke, I was an only-when-drinking smoker. Being in denial that I was a smoker, I grabbed Don's cigarettes.

One day he said, "That's it! I haven't said anything for a long time, but I'm getting sick of you taking my cigarettes. They're expensive, and sometimes I only have a few left, and when you ask me for one, it gives me anxiety."

"I'm sorry," I told him. "You are absolutely right. I've been in denial. I thought that if I never bought a pack of my own, I could keep convincing myself that I'm not a smoker."

Don had moved into my building, and the 7-Eleven was half a block away. I marched up there and bought a carton of Newport menthols for Don and a single pack of Marlboro Lights for me. I looked at the pack of Marlboro Lights on the counter and couldn't believe I was actually buying a pack of cigarettes. On the walk back to the condos, I couldn't stop thinking about the fact that I'd just bought a pack of cigarettes.

I was a smoker.

Recommendation:

For the next thirty years, I quit smoking many times. Several times, I would quit for years. I once went for four years without smoking. In 2015, I read the book *The Easy Way to Quit Smoking* by Alan Carr. I finished the book one evening and thought, *That was a joke. What am I supposed to do now?* I put the book down on the table next to the sofa and went to bed. The next morning, I woke up and didn't crave a cigarette. I haven't had a cigarette since then and have no desire to smoke. The book is awesome, and I recommend it, but I believe God looked out for me as well. To this day, I have no desire to smoke.

8

WHERE IS MY LIFE GOING?

Being a sprinter at Georgia Tech was fun. It kept me in great shape, and we traveled to some amazing places. One of my favorite places was Furman University in Greenville, South Carolina. Furman hosted the Tom Black Classic Track Meet. Furman was the most beautiful place I'd ever seen. There were mature trees and rolling hills with green grass. A large lake was perfectly placed in the middle of the campus. I couldn't get enough. Every year, I wanted to stay there and not leave.

We traveled to Tennessee, Florida, Alabama, Virginia, and other states. During the height of the season, I worked out seven days a week. I ran, lifted weights, stretched my legs, etc. I focused on not getting injured. Practicing high hurdles—forty-two inches high—and intermediate hurdles—thirty-six inches high—offered more than enough chances to get injured. One misstep or slight loss of balance, and I would crash to the ground. I broke my fair share of hurdles and injured my foot or knee more than once.

When I arrived in Miami in 1982, I wanted to stay in shape. I joined a gym to lift weights. I jogged around my neighborhood a lot, but I wanted to sprint. There were several running clubs, but they mostly ran long distances. I hated running long distances. I found the Sunshine Striders Track Club, an Amateur Athletic Union (AAU) club. In the spring, they held several track meets in the South Florida area. There weren't enough participants interested in hurdles to compete as a hurdler, but they had the 100-meter, 200-meter, and 400-meter sprints. I physically matured in my early twenties, and my second year in the club, I ran my personal best 100 meters at 10.7 seconds.

I stuck with it for three years. As my job responsibilities increased and I entered the University of Miami night school in 1983 to get a Master of Science in Industrial Engineering, I didn't have time to stay in competitive shape. But while I was in the Sunshine Striders, two things happened. I got to hang out with like-minded people, and the commitment to the club motivated me to stay in top physical condition.

I was lucky to get hired into an organization that brought ten to twelve college graduates into the group every six months. I was fortunate because my first job out of Georgia Tech placed me on a team of thirty to forty recent college graduates. It was fun, but it was also a proving ground. If you were in this group for over a year, it was an indication you were not that impressive. I was promoted out in nine months. In those nine months, I built some amazing relationships with people my age.

Recommendation:

Put people in your life who will hold you accountable. It can be direct or indirect. I joined the Sunshine Striders as a way to hold myself accountable. I knew there were going to be track meets every couple of weeks. There was a coach who expected me to stay in shape and be a part of the team. There were teammates counting on me to score points for the team.

I took the Graduate Record Examination (GRE) and was accepted into the University of Miami graduate school. Knowing I had to get good grades for FPL to pay my tuition held me accountable.

Put people in your life who will hold you accountable. It can be direct or indirect.

In grad school, I met a girl who was on the women's golf team. I'll call her Lizzie.

I'd say, "Lizzie, let's go to the beach Saturday."

Lizzie would say, "I can't. I have to go to the range and hit balls Saturday."

"Okay. Can we go out after?"

"Well, I'm going to be hitting balls all day. Afterward, I'll be exhausted, and I'll need to go home and rest."

"Can I come over and hang out with you?"

"I would prefer to recover. How about we get together Sunday?"

Her golf coach and teammates held her accountable. She took responsibility and worked hard. Lizzie went on to be an LPGA pro golfer.

Many recovery programs have it built into their routine for you to have an accountability partner; it's called a sponsor in AA. This person helps you understand how the program works and encourages you to stay with it. Find good accountability partners.

Living Day to Day

I lived day by day. I bounced along, struggled with life, and didn't have a clear direction or know what I wanted to do.

Frequently on Friday afternoons, with no notice at all, Don would say, "Let's go to the Keys."

All I had to do was say yes, and we were off and driving. We never knew where we were going to end up or what we were going to do.

We stopped to fill the gas tank and buy beer. It took us about an hour to reach Key Largo, the first of the keys. The keys are a 113-mile chain of coral and limestone islands connected by forty-two bridges, with one bridge that is seven miles long. The last key is Key West. It takes three hours to drive from Key Largo to Key West on a two-lane road, US Highway 1. One morning every year, they shut down the bridge for the Seven Mile Bridge Run.

Once we hit Key Largo, Don would ask, "So, what do you want to do?"

"Let's go fishing."

"Okay, I think I know a place we can go."

"Let's go snorkeling."

"Yeah, I know exactly the place to go. Or we could go to that bar in Islamorada."

"If we start at the bar, we'll never go fishing or snorkeling."

"Oh, yeah. Well, we'll figure it out."

We had hours to decide. All we cared about at the moment was drinking beer and playing the music loud. When we liked the song, we'd sing along at the top of our lungs. We always figured out something to do, and we always had a blast.

On some of the trips, we would stop at a few bars along the way and find ourselves at the southernmost key, Key West. Key West was one of my favorite places. Ernest Hemingway had a home there, and there were large estates with tennis courts. It was the end of US Highway 1, the southernmost point in the United States. I was never bored on Duval Street, and at the end of the day, everyone gathered to watch the sunset, serenaded by a bagpipe player in Scottish garb. Don and I would secure accommodations and finish the night at Sloppy Joe's on Duval Street. It was Ernest Hemingway's favorite bar in the 1930s.

Our trips served to pass the time, and we didn't worry about anything except making sure one of us was sober enough to drive home. On Monday, I'd go back to my job, and Don would go back to the salon where he worked as a successful hairdresser. Neither one of us gave a lot of thought to where our lives were headed.

Write It Down

My therapist, Nellie, asked me to start writing down my goals. I'd become an expert at helping Florida Power and Light develop and write down the company's goals, and for my master's thesis, I researched how to create and execute a strategic plan for large and small companies. For some reason, my research work never translated to me personally until Nellie suggested I write where I wanted to be in three years. I struggled with that. I had no idea where I wanted to be tomorrow, much less in three years.

I now write my goals for one year, three years, and ten years. Research has proven that people who are intentional and write down their goals versus bouncing through life live a more fulfilling life.

I suggest you write down your goals.

Procrastination

I've had a problem with procrastination my whole life. When I started graduate school in 1983, I had two choices. I could either do coursework and get my degree, or I could choose a combination of courses and write a thesis. Being the ambitious soul that I am, of course I wanted the glamour of writing a thesis. Big mistake. With coursework, you attend class, complete homework, do projects, and take exams. All of this was on a tight, rigid schedule. It forced me to keep up and get things done.

For my thesis, I was on my own. At first, I jumped in, but then as time went on, my interest started to fade. Furthermore, I made the mistake of asking professors from the Industrial Engineering College and the Business School to sit on my thesis committee. In my update meetings, they spent more than half the time in arguments with each other about who was correct when giving me guidance on how to move to the next step. When they bickered, it made me even less interested in completing my work. I would rather clean my oven than make progress on my thesis.

When I met my wife, Jan, she whipped me into shape. I was used to letting my dishes overflow in the sink until they fell over before I washed them. My bills would pile high on my kitchen table, and I wouldn't pay them until they fell over. Whenever I wanted to change clothes, I left a trail of clothes on the floor of my condo for days instead of hanging them up or putting them in the laundry pile. The laundry pile would get about four to five feet high before I did laundry. The master bedroom had two walk-in closets. I used one for clothes and the other one for piling up the laundry when I bothered to pick it up off the floor.

Jan helped me get my act together. We were married in 1991, and I am still a work in progress, but I am light-years ahead of where I was. On Saturdays, Jan encouraged me to go to the library for four hours to work on my thesis. In hindsight, the regimen of a schedule and deadlines worked. It was no surprise. I got back in the groove, and in less than a year, I finished my thesis and graduated. In total, it took me four years to complete my thesis.

Recommendation:

Set a goal of zero procrastination. Even if you have your life 100 percent together, you'll still have difficulty achieving zero procrastination. If you were a monk in a temple, you'd still have chores. I can't think of a way to attain the goal of zero procrastination, but I still think it's a good goal. Most people have so many things going on at once that it's impossible not to put off some things.

If you know you're going to procrastinate, how do you handle it? The answer is to prioritize. Let your "no" mean no—to yourself and to others.

> All you need to say is simply "Yes" or "No"; anything beyond this comes from the evil one."
>
> Matthew 5:37

Don't let others push you around and get you to do things you don't want to do. It's simple advice to tell you to just say yes or no, but it's not so easy to do it. Remember that you don't owe anyone an explanation. You decide for yourself how to spend your time.

9

WHAT IS YOUR PURPOSE?

When I prayed for Jesus to come into my life, it felt like a small bolt of lightning hit my heart. It was supernatural. For an instant, it took my breath away. I had no idea what had happened to me. Looking back, I describe it as if I was surrounded by blackness and someone from above dripped a single white dot of paint on a dark surface. The white drip splattered as it hit the surface. It was small compared to the vast darkness. However, the white kept growing. The white is still growing.

Did I never have a sinful thought again? Of course! I hear people say all the time, "Christians are hypocrites." Christians are human. We are people on a journey through this world who have made a commitment. We believe that Jesus was the son of God, that He died for our sins, and that we are on a never-ending journey to be better today than we were yesterday. That process is called sanctification.

Does it mean I will never sin again? No. Does that mean I may be perceived as a hypocrite? Absolutely. I'm not here to judge you, but do I judge people? Every day. I'm not here to put my desires above yours, but do I put my desires above yours? Every day. I'm not here to sin against you, but do I do that? Every day.

I believe I'm here to serve you, love you, forgive you, and accept you. I pray for God to use my mind, my heart, my body, and my assets to serve him. I'm giving him everything I have. Everything I have first came from God. It all belongs to him anyway. I will die someday, and my body will return to dust. I can't bring anything with me. I believe I'll go to heaven, where I will be given a new body and live eternally with God.

Recommendation:

> Those who live according to the flesh have their minds set on what the flesh desires; but those who live in accordance with the Spirit have their minds set on what the Spirit desires. The mind governed by the flesh is death, but the mind governed by the Spirit is life and peace. The mind governed by the flesh is hostile to God; it does not submit to God's law, nor can it do so. Those who are in the realm of the flesh cannot please God.
>
> You, however, are not in the realm of the flesh but are in the realm of the Spirit, if indeed the Spirit of God lives in you. And if anyone does not have the Spirit of Christ, they do not belong to Christ. But if Christ is in you, then even though your body is subject to death because of sin, the Spirit gives life because of righteousness. And if the Spirit of him who raised Jesus from the dead is living in you, he who raised Christ from the dead will also give life to your mortal bodies because of his Spirit who lives in you.
>
> Romans 8:5-11

When I first read the Bible or heard my pastor talk about how we should live our lives, it sounded like punishment to follow the guidelines. Yet every time I changed my life to follow scripture, my life was better. I try to live a God-centered life. It's the best choice I have made.

Have You Found Yourself?

I don't have any medical research or scientific research to back this up, but I believe that for most of us, when we take our first breath, we are the most whole we'll ever be from a mental standpoint. We just came from our mother's womb, where it was warm, where we were fed, and all our needs were met. We were made in the image of God. From the moment of our birth, imperfect people influenced our mental and physical conditions. Research says that 90 percent of who we will be for the rest of our lives is set in place before age ten. God, family, school, friends, our home, our neighborhood all play a role in who we are.

All my life, I've heard people say, "I need to find myself." For many of us, somewhere between the ages of eighteen and twenty-eight, we'll be flung into the world with no instruction manual. It's no surprise that some people can't find themselves. Satan tempted Jesus. He took him to a high place and said, "Look around. I will give you everything you see if you will just follow me." Jesus told him to get lost.

You don't need to get right to come to Jesus. You come to Jesus to get right.

> In the garden at Gethsemane, just hours before he was taken to be crucified, Jesus struggled. Going a little farther, he fell with his face to the ground and prayed, "My Father, if it is possible, may this cup be taken from me. Yet not as I will, but as you will."
>
> Matthew 26:39

Three times Jesus prayed this prayer: "My Father, if it is possible, may this cup be taken from me. Yet not as I will, but as you will." Throughout the Bible, Jesus shows he was well aware that he came to take away the sins of the world. Jesus gave his life to save my life. In the final hour, Jesus, who was both God and man, prayed to his father to see if the crucifixion could be taken off his shoulders.

I would be terrified to face the burden of being tortured and crucified. The human side of Jesus asked his Father to lift the burden. Jesus could have easily stopped the entire episode himself. He didn't. He went through an awful death and took on the sins of all humanity. I cannot imagine what Jesus went through to save my life. Can you imagine someone loving you so much that they willingly sacrificed their own life to save yours?

Recommendation:

I've also heard people say, "I don't know what my purpose is." My own answer is that I try my best to serve God. I believe my purpose is to surrender to God. To be obedient to God. To worship God. I believe that by doing this, I can be a light for people in darkness and can love people and care for others. You don't need to get right to come to Jesus. You come to Jesus to get right.

It's Not All About You

I wanted to be a millionaire by age thirty. I wanted money, promotions, partying, sex, etc. When I accepted Jesus, my life changed. I was a twenty-five-year-old man, yet I was an infant in Christ. I'm still trying to let go of this world. I know I've made progress, and I believe it's a lifelong journey. I pray every day that God will use me to love people. Use things, love people. Not the other way around.

Recommendation:

> For whoever wants to save their life will lose it, but whoever loses their life for me and for the gospel will save it. What good is it for someone to gain the whole world, yet forfeit their soul? Or what can anyone give in exchange for their soul?
>
> Mark 8:35-37

Nothing you do can earn God's love and grace. There's no price tag on Jesus. You can't buy it; you can't earn it; it is free. The one requirement is that you believe that Jesus is the Son of God and he died on the cross for your sins. It sounds impossible, but as I and millions of others can attest, it's not impossible. Let Jesus into your heart.

10

UNFULFILLED LONGING

In 1984, after about eighteen months on the job at Florida Power and Light, I was promoted to the position of Transmission and Distribution Service Planner. Mary had been promoted to Service Planner Manager in the North Dade service area, and she asked me to come work with her. I loved Mary and agreed without hesitation. She had also pulled some of the other talented engineers in to join her team. There were probably ten people on her team who'd graduated college within the last two to four years. Vic Arena was the Senior Service Planner. He was a little older, was married, and had two kids. On occasion, we got Vic to behave as irresponsibly as us, the young engineers.

We didn't do it often, but sometimes we'd get together and party. One Friday, we agreed to meet for lunch at one of our favorite pizza spots. I'm not sure who suggested we get "just one" round of beers—which led to ordering pitchers of beer. Next thing we knew, it was after 4:00 p.m. Mary gave us a lot of latitude, but if ten of us didn't return to the office on a Friday afternoon, she'd be upset.

"We have to go back to the office," someone said.

"No way, we can't go back to work," someone else said.

"We have to," we all agreed.

We devised a plan in minutes. We all went to the nearest drug store, and each of us purchased $1 sunglasses and a pack of mint Tic-Tacs. We raced to the office and met at the entrance in the back of the building. Each of us threw a handful of Tic-Tacs in our mouth, put on our sunglasses, and started marching up the stairs. By 4:50, we were all at our desks. Mary was in her office with the door closed. There was no way she didn't hear us marching up the steps. We snickered and whispered back and forth. We thought that if she didn't come out of her office, we would have gotten away with our Friday afternoon shenanigans.

At 4:55 p.m., Mary opened her door. She looked across the room and saw us all at our desks wearing cheap sunglasses. She leaned on her doorframe and tried to figure out what was going on. After a long pause, she said, "Is everything all right?"

My friend Dave was the best at keeping a straight face, so he piped up.

"Yeah, sure, everything's all right."

Mary made a face like she wasn't sure what to think or if she believed Dave. She drew out her response.

"Ooo-kaay," she said, as she slowly rolled off the doorframe, went back into her office, and closed her door.

We couldn't believe that was it. Our eyes focused on the clock on the wall. As soon as it ticked five o'clock, we all bolted for the stairwell, almost knocking each other over. We busted out laughing as we ran down the stairs and went back to the pizza place for a few more hours.

I thought we'd had a blast drinking beer. A few weeks later, I invited the whole team to my new condo, which wasn't far from the office. My refrigerator was packed with Budweisers. As Friday approached, people asked me what the plan was.

"We're going to drink some beers!" I responded.

Friday rolled around, and I was very excited. But nobody showed up. I was devastated. I spent that weekend coming up with all kinds of conspiracies to explain their absence. I almost didn't want to go to work Monday morning. I'd tried something new, and it was an epic fail.

Monday morning, everyone was in the office. They all seemed normal. If there had been a conspiracy, they all played along well.

"Hey, Dave, you weren't able to make it Friday?" I asked.

"What was Friday?"

"I invited everyone over for a few beers."

"Oh, hey man, I'm sorry. I had a date with my girlfriend."

I felt like he was sincere.

"Hey, Vic, you weren't able to make it Friday?" I asked.

"Are you kidding? I had to pick my son up from school and take my daughter to a friend's birthday party. There was no way I could make it."

Vic also seemed sincere.

"Hey Barbara, you weren't able to make it Friday?"

"Well, I called Deb, and she couldn't go, and I didn't want to go by myself. I live on Key Biscayne, and it would have been a long trip. I'm sorry I couldn't make it."

Remember, there were no smartphones back then. The only way anyone could have communicated with me was by calling my home phone. Since I'd just moved in, no one had my phone number written in their phone books.

Recommendation:

I was so relieved that the reason nobody came to my party was that they all had busy lives. I didn't feel like anyone was mean-spirited or hadn't shown up to spite me. I'd tried something new and failed. Don't be afraid to try new things.

I also realized that I often try to do things all by myself. I had made the party about me. Imagine if I had involved two or three teammates. I could have said, "I just moved into my new condo and want to have a get-together, you know, like a housewarming party. How do you think I should go about it?" The result would have been different. Take a chance, try new things, and learn from every new journey.

Figure Out What You Want

When I was sixteen, it was perfectly legal for me to leave home and quit school if I wanted to. I was desperate to get out of my house and live on my own. But where would I go? How would I survive? There were too many unanswered questions in my mind. I decided to hang in there until I went off to college.

I grew up in the streets, with many temptations to break the law. One thing that kept me focused was my dream to be an SR71 pilot. The SR71 was a US Air Force spy plane that flew over 1,000 miles per hour. If my friends thought about doing something stupid, all I had to say to myself was, *I'm not giving up my dream for this.* My friends knew being a pilot was so important to me that it would be a waste of their breath to try to talk me into taking part in their mischief. I knew that if I got arrested, any chance of me getting into the Air Force Academy (AFA) would be ruined.

For close to a year, I worked through my congressman, Henry Helstoski, to get a nomination for the United States Air Force Academy. I remember being intimidated by him. I was a poor boy from New Jersey, and he was a US congressman. Why would he help me?

But that didn't stop me. I had to go to the library to research how to apply for the nomination. I had to fill out forms, write essays, and mail in documents. I had a phone interview with the congressman.

I got the nomination! I received paperwork in the mail that said to go to a medical facility for a physical and to plan to be there all day. I was poked and prodded, had blood drawn, and gave a urine sample. They did x-rays, looked at my eyes and teeth, and checked my hearing, flexibility, and strength. It took the entire day.

Being nominated wasn't the end of the line. I didn't realize the academy also had to accept me. They assigned a liaison officer to me, who I'll call Kyle, who scheduled an appointment to come to my house. He delivered the paperwork I needed to get a cavity repaired and have my dentist sign, and I needed to have more x-rays of my lower back taken to send to the Air Force doctors. It took a few weeks to get these tasks done.

When I'd been a sophomore in high school, I had a high-speed accident on my bicycle. I flipped head over heels three or four times and ended up in the hospital. They discovered I had Spondylolisthesis L4/L5. My spine had two small broken bones that held the L4 and L5 vertebra in place. As a result, my spine had shifted over many years. I was nervous that the academy doctors wouldn't like what they saw.

Humility is not thinking less of yourself; it is thinking of yourself less.

After what seemed like forever, I received a letter in the mail that said I was not accepted into the Air Force Academy. For years, my dream had been to fly the SR71. It took nearly a year of hard work to get nominated. One sheet of paper in the mail, and it all came crashing down. I was devastated. I cried. It was a crushing blow, like a hard punch in the stomach.

I regained my composure and called Kyle. He picked up the phone, and I said, "Kyle, I got rejected by the academy."

"What?" he replied. "I'm so sorry I didn't see this first. Can I call you right back?"

"Sure."

Within a few minutes, Kyle called me back. "Can I come over to meet with you?" he asked.

"Sure."

Kyle arrived in his Air Force uniform—always crisp and put together. He was a great guy, and we had grown to be friends.

"You passed the physical exam with flying colors," he said. "But since you expressed an interest in being accepted into flight school, they decided you couldn't get into a cockpit with your back the way it is."

"But I played football, and I've been on the varsity track team for three years. I'm strong and physically fit. I don't get it."

Kyle leaned in. "Imagine for a moment there are two of you. You as you are now and the other you without the issue with your back. Who would you choose to put in a $4 million plane that could have bombs strapped to it?"

I did not want to give him an honest answer. It took me a moment to answer. "I suppose the perfect me."

"Correct."

Kyle went on to say, "I've seen this many times before. With your file, we could appeal, and you'd get into the academy.

But you wouldn't get into the flight school. You could be a helicopter pilot, maybe."

Helicopter pilot! My dream was to fly the SR71. By design, it leaked fluid on the ground so that when it was tens of thousands of feet in the air, it could expand without damaging itself. It flew so fast the speed was classified. Somewhere between 1,000 and 2,000 miles per hour. A helicopter—no way!

"If I can't get into flight school, I don't want to go," I replied.

"I know how hard you've worked and how important this is to you," Kyle said. "Right now, you're emotional, and I understand that. I'm not going to take that as your final answer. I'll give you a week to think it over. Does that sound okay with you?"

For the next week, it was all I could think about. The chances of being an SR71 pilot were slim to none. I knew that going in. I thought that if I didn't make the SR71 pilot slot, I could step back and try to be a fighter pilot. Still, a fighter pilot wasn't a sure thing, but I knew the risks, and I would have taken them for a shot at being a pilot. To be told I would never get in a cockpit before I even set foot on campus destroyed my dream. I decided not to pursue the Air Force Academy.

Recommendation:

Things won't always go your way, but it's important to strive toward your dreams. Until I was twenty-five years old, my dreams focused on me conquering the world. After I accepted Jesus and the Holy Spirit into my heart, I fell in love with the Word of God and began to realize I was put here to serve others. Many people who know me can attest that I still pursued worldly rewards. To this day, I still fight the current of the world trying to push me off course. It is a lifelong journey, and it isn't easy.

> And why do you worry about your clothes? See how the flowers of the fields grow. They do not labor or spin. Yet I tell you that not even Solomon in all his splendor was dressed like one of these. If that is how God clothes the grass of the field, which is here today and tomorrow is thrown into the fire, will he not much more clothe you—you of little faith? So do not worry, saying, "What shall we eat?" or "What shall we drink?" or "What shall we wear?" For pagans run after all these things, and your heavenly Father knows that you need them. But seek his kingdom and his righteousness, and all these things will be given to you as well. Therefore, do not worry about tomorrow, for tomorrow will worry about itself. Each day has enough trouble of its own.
>
> Matthew 6:28-34

As long as you are breathing, you need to dream. Lay your dreams at the feet of God. Seek God's kingdom and his righteousness. All else will follow. Humility is not thinking less of yourself; it is thinking of yourself less.

Get Help

> While Americans of all ages are feeling the emotional toll of the pandemic, millennials represent a particularly vulnerable group. They were already suffering from declining mental health, leading to what experts call a "health shock." The new normal is expected to inflame the loneliness and anxiety that so many within the generation already felt.
>
> All generations have reported feelings of depression and anxiety during the pandemic, but it's most experienced by

> millennials, those born between 1981 and 1996, and Gen Z, those born in 1997 and beyond.[1]

It's no secret that it's difficult to live alone. Loneliness can be difficult, and I experienced it a great deal after my divorce.

In the mid-1980s in Miami, I was unhappy in my marriage. I decided I wanted to get divorced. In Florida, you had to be separated for one year before you could file for divorce. Lawyers put together separation papers, and after a year of separation, we filed for divorce. We didn't have any children, but we had three dogs. We met in court, and a judge wanted to make sure we were both okay to move forward. The lawyers hashed out a divorce agreement, and we were both fine with it.

As the judge looked through the divorce decree, she popped her head up and said, "I was under the impression that there were no children!" She looked at us wide-eyed, waiting for someone to reply.

I looked at my attorney. I looked at my soon-to-be ex-wife. The attorneys looked at each other. I don't know which attorney spoke up, but one of them said, "Your Honor, that is correct. There are no children in this marriage."

"Well then, who are Jacqueline Sheridor, Romeo Sheridor, and . . ." Her voice trailed off as she finished the sentence. "... Juliet Sheridor?" As if she were talking to herself, she said under her breath, "Who in their right mind names children Romeo and Juliet?" She popped her head up again.

---

1 Hillary Hoffower, "The 'loneliest generation' gets lonelier: How millennials are dealing with the anxieties of isolation and the uncertainties of life after quarantine," Business Insider, May 31, 2020, https://www.businessinsider.com/millennial-mental-health-coronavirus-pandemic-quarantine-2020-5.

We all laughed. "Those are the dogs, Your Honor," someone said. The judge laughed too.

We had three AKC-registered Labrador Retrievers. My wife and I bred Labrador Retrievers, and it was a tradition to give the dogs a last name that combined the owners' name and the breed. "Sheri" was the first part of my last name, and the "dor" was the last part of Labrador; hence "Sheridor" was the last name that appeared on their registrations. The agreement said I would get Romeo and Juliet, and my ex would get Jacqueline.

Be more than a conqueror through Jesus who loves you.

As part of the agreement, I had to get out of the condo while a sheriff let my ex-wife in to get the things, which the divorce decree said she was entitled to. After she left, Romeo was there, and I searched everywhere for Juliet. She was gone. My ex had taken Juliet and my new 35mm camera, both specified in the court order as belonging to me. I was upset, but I was so glad it was all over that I didn't fight it.

I sat on my sofa and stared at the TV, which was turned off. Romeo sat on the carpet in front of me and looked at me as if to say, "Dad, what is going on?" My eyes filled with tears, which started running down my face. Romeo didn't care about the rules; he climbed up on the sofa and put his head in my lap. I sat there for hours, numb and crying. I thought to myself, *What just happened?*

I was divorced. I felt like a huge failure. I realized I had to take responsibility for my part. Fifty percent of my divorce was my fault. Shortly after this, I found Nellie, my therapist. During the same four years that Nellie and I worked on me, God worked on me as well, and God is still working on me today.

Recommendation:

If you are struggling, don't be afraid to get help. Be more than a conqueror through Jesus who loves you.The number of resources available for whatever is troubling you are endless. Without God, I would be dead or in prison. Of that, I have no doubt.

> Who shall separate us from the love of Christ? Shall trouble or hardship or persecution or famine or nakedness or danger or sword? As it is written:
>
> For your sake we face death all day long:
> we are considered as sheep to slaughter.
>
> No, in all these things we are more than conquerors through him who loved us. For I am convinced that neither death nor life, neither angels nor demons, neither the present nor the future, nor any powers, neither height nor depth, nor anything else in all creation, will be able to separate us from the love of God that is in Christ Jesus our Lord.
>
> Romans 8:35-39

Be more than a conqueror through Jesus, who loves you.

11

SO, YOU WANT TO HAVE SEX!

I'm not a therapist, and for that matter, I am not an expert on sexuality. I will go out on a limb and say that as a young adult, your sex drive is stronger than it will ever be. In college, I had a fraternity brother, who I'll call Walter. Walter was not shy about telling us his goal in life was to sleep with 1,000 women before he got married.

We were members of the Lambda Chi Alpha fraternity on the campus of Georgia Tech. There were about 125 brothers. We had a nice house where fifty-five guys could live. It had four floors with large, white columns across the front. We had a basketball court and patio on one side. Through the main entrance, there was a large, formal living room, and there was also a large dining room that could seat 125 on the ground floor. Since many sororities didn't have large houses, we allowed the girlfriends of the brothers to buy into our meal plan.

Monday through Friday, we offered two sittings for lunch and two sittings for dinner.

Every waking moment, Walter was obsessed with sleeping with women. At one point, no one wanted to share a room with him because he always brought girls to his room and kicked out his roommate. Halfway through one year, his roommate had had enough. He lost it. "I am sick and tired of getting kicked out of my room. Next time, I'm not leaving," he said. Walter apologized, "You're right. I'm sorry. I'll try to do better going forward." It was enough to take the tension out of the moment, but Walter didn't change. I don't think he was capable. Late one night, there was an incident where Walter asked his roommate to get out of the room, and he refused. They almost came to blows. Walter, being Walter, convinced the young woman to have sex with him even though his roommate was still in the room.

This is an extreme example of what I would call an unrealistic sex drive. From my experience and from observing my friends, we all had a healthy sex drive. However, I never met any other guy in my life who wanted to have sex with 1,000 women before he got married.

Recommendation:

> Flee from sexual immorality. All other sins a person commits are outside the body, but whoever sins sexually, sins against their own body. Do you not know that your bodies are temples of the Holy Spirit, who is in you, whom you have received from God? You are not your own, you were bought at a price. Therefore, honor God with your bodies.
>
> 1 Corinthians 6:18-20

From my experience, being sexually intimate with someone changes things. It changes both people because it's personal and intimate. You're giving something of yourself that you would never share with the hundreds of people you meet throughout your day. Sex is magnificent, a gift from God, and God tells us to share it with our spouse. I believe God's way is always the path to the best life you can live.

And remember this: You can never undo having sex with someone.

Don't Drink or Use Drugs

> You, my brothers and sisters, were called to be free. But do not use your freedom to indulge the flesh; rather serve one another humbly in love. For the entire law is fulfilled in keeping this one command: "Love your neighbor as yourself." If you bite and devour each other, watch out or you will be destroyed by each other.
>
> So I say, walk by the Spirit, and you will not gratify the desires of the flesh. For the flesh desires what is contrary to the Spirit, and the Spirit what is contrary to the flesh. They are in conflict with each other, so that you are not to do whatever you want. But if you are led by the Spirit, you are not under the law.
>
> The acts of the flesh are obvious: sexual immorality, impurity and debauchery; idolatry and witchcraft; hatred, discord, jealousy, fits of rage, selfish ambition, dissensions, factions, and envy; drunkenness, orgies, and the like. I warn you, as I did before, that those who live like this will not inherit the kingdom of God.
>
> But the fruit of the Spirit is love, joy, peace, forbearance, kindness, goodness, faithfulness, gentleness and self-control. Against such things there is no law. Those who belong to Christ

> Jesus have crucified the flesh with its passions and desires. Since we live by the Spirit, let us keep in step with the Spirit. Let us not become conceited, provoking and envying each other.
>
> Galatians 5:13-26

I've attended parties in public settings, bars, and nightclubs. I've attended private parties at friends' homes, the fraternity house, hotels, wedding venues, and other places where the general public was not invited. The longer the night went on, the more I drank, and sometimes I'd use drugs. On more than one occasion, I'd leave with a woman and have sex—a woman I'd never met before. I'm ashamed and embarrassed to admit this. I'd wake up the next morning and think to myself, *What was I thinking?* I believe that for the majority of people, we know when something doesn't feel right.

Having a one-night stand with a stranger never felt right to me. I know for a fact that if drugs and alcohol weren't in the picture, it never would have happened. The reason I know this is because I've never met a stranger and had sex with her within a few hours unless drugs and alcohol were involved.

Recommendation:

I sound like a hypocrite because I am a hypocrite. I'm telling you that if I could go back and live my life again, I would have wanted to follow God's guidance. I wouldn't have used alcohol and drugs or had sex before marriage. I've had troubles and heartache because I couldn't surrender to God, control my desires, and live a righteous life. I don't want you to face what I faced. Love yourself, love others, love God, and accept the love of God.

Peer Pressure

St. Michaels Catholic Monastery in Union City, New Jersey, occupied six square blocks, and on its campus was one of the most beautiful churches I've ever seen. The grounds around the facilities were immaculate. There was a lawn as far as the eye could see and large trees and walking paths throughout the property. Around the perimeter, there was a combination stone wall and wrought iron fence. It must have been ten feet tall.

As kids, we'd push each other up and help one another climb the fence. We'd play football in the open grassy space. About half the time, we played until we got exhausted and left. The other half of the time, a priest dressed in a black gown from neck to shoes would walk toward us from the monastery. He'd walk slowly, head down, knowing we could see him coming. Nobody had to say a word. We ran for the fence and climbed over it as quickly as we could before the priest got too close.

On the corner of the property farthest away from the monastery and church, St. Michael's created a blacktop area and installed a full-court basketball court. The neighborhood kids, and sometimes adults, played there every night, barring bad weather. One of our high school classmates wanted to celebrate his eighteenth birthday.

He said, "Let's meet at the basketball court. We could play hoops for a while and then buy some beer." I'll call the birthday boy Vinny.

There were about six or seven of us there, and we had fun playing hoops. It started to get dark, and even though the lights would soon turn on automatically, we decided we'd had enough basketball. We agreed that we'd all chip in money to buy Vinny a quart of beer—and we'd each get one, too, to celebrate his birthday. Judging from what happened next, I'm not sure that Vinny had ever had a beer before. In 1977, eighteen was the legal age to drink beer in New York, and it was Vinny's eighteenth birthday.

When Vinny had almost finished his quart of beer, he started to cry a deep belly cry.

"Vinny, it's okay. Beer has a way of making you lose it. You'll be okay," John said. John and I were close friends, and we were worried about Vinny.

"I'm okay. I'll be fine," Vinny said, as he pulled himself together.

A few minutes later, and after a few more sips of beer, Vinny began to cry even harder. Now our anxiety kicked up a notch.

I asked, "Hey Vinny, what's going on, man? It's your birthday. We're celebrating your eighteenth birthday. It's supposed to be a fun time. What's going on, man?"

"I'm a loser. I'm a failure. I'm going to kill myself."

John and I looked at each other, perplexed. We whispered to each other, "What's wrong with him?"

John put his arm around Vinny and walked him away from the group. One on one, John asked Vinny, "What is going on? Why are you crying so hard? What's this crazy talk about you killing yourself? Please tell me what's going on."

Vinny answered, "I'm eighteen years old, and I'm still a virgin."

While John and Vinny talked, the other guys said, "Vinny's freaking us out. We're taking off."

John walked Vinny back to where I was, and they told me the problem. We spent about an hour with Vinny and told him it wasn't a big deal that he was a virgin.

He asked, "Are either of you virgins?"

We both confessed, "No, we're not." That set the conversation back quite a bit.

Vinny started crying again. He yelled, "See? See what I mean? Neither of you are virgins!"

You have nothing to prove to your peers.

After a while, the combination of John and me not giving up and the alcohol wearing off, Vinny calmed down. We walked him home and waited for him to go inside.

Neither of us thought this was funny. The peer pressure to have sex is powerful, and it's real.

Recommendation:

> When I was a child, I talked like a child, I thought like a child, I reasoned like a child. When I became a man, I put the ways of childhood behind me.
>
> 1 Corinthians 13:11

No matter what your age, peer pressure never goes away. I felt a tremendous amount of peer pressure to have sex when I was a teenager. I was seventeen the first time, but I encourage you to wait until you're married.

You have nothing to prove to your peers.

12

CHOOSING A PARTNER

Wow! This is a big one. How do I coach young adults about how to pick the right person? Whenever I have a question, I like to turn to the Bible for answers. But before I do, I want to make it clear that celibacy (not having sexual relations), marriage, and sex are gifts from God and are to be celebrated in the right context.

> Now for the matters you wrote about: it is good for a man not to marry.
>
> 1 Corinthians 7

Some people receive the gift of celibacy. For that individual, God alone is enough, and God fulfills that person. I wasn't called to live this way. However, the closer I get to God, the more I understand how it's possible to be completely fulfilled by God.

1 Corinthians 7 continues:

> . . . But since there is so much immorality, each man should have his own wife, and each woman her own husband. The husband should fulfill his marital duty to his wife, and likewise the wife to her husband.

God doesn't want us to engage in sexual immorality. Marriage and sex are gifts from God. He wants us to marry, and it's okay to embrace the joys of a sexual relationship under the bonds of marriage. I've already told you that I had sexual relations before I was married, so I'm not here to judge anyone. But if I could have a do-over, I'd want to remain celibate until I was married. First, because it's the will of God, and second, because I could have avoided a lot of heartache and pain.

Do you have a friend or family member who always seems to pick the wrong person? You see it, others see it, but they don't. They make the same mistake over and over again. What makes us do that? Are we wired wrong? Is it damage or baggage from our parents? I don't know. In my case, I selected partners based on physical attraction. Within one or two weeks, I'd figure out if it was going to work or not, and that was it. Some other relationships went on much longer. I'll break my relationship history down into three scenarios:

> *Whenever I have a question, I like to turn to the Bible for answers.*

Scenario One: She liked me more than I liked her.

I never did like this scenario. One day, I walked back to my dorm from class. A classmate I didn't know was waiting at the top of the hill.

She said, "Hello," in a pleasant voice.

A little taken off guard, I looked at her and wondered if I should know her. I didn't, but I stopped and said, "Hello."

The girl I'll call Kelsey said, "Do you mind if I walk you down the hill?" Georgia Tech has a long, steep hill that goes from the front of the library and classroom buildings down past fraternity row. At the bottom of the hill are the dormitories.

"Sure."

We chatted; it was a nice conversation. At the entrance to my dorm, we said goodbye.

The next day, Kelsey was at the top of the hill again. This went on for a few days. On the third or fourth day, she slipped her hand in mine on the way down the hill. It was nice to feel the touch of another person in a caring way.

The next day, Kelsey wasn't at the top of the hill. I was surprised. I still wasn't sure how I felt. We'd only met a few days before, so I tried not to think too much about it. I got to my dorm, and as I walked down the hall, I could see that my door was open. At this time of day, my roommate was in class, so I was a little surprised. I thought he'd forgotten to close the door. When I pushed open the door, I saw Kelsey sitting at my desk. I was in shock.

"Wow, how did you get in here?"

"Your roommate let me in."

She could tell I was a little upset. We'd just met a few days ago, and all of a sudden, she was in my room? Over the course of the next few days, I thought about how I could get out of this.

Kelsey wanted to have sex. I wasn't sure about having sex, but what did I do? You guessed it—we had sex. That just made things worse. Within a week, I broke things off with her and felt ashamed that I'd had sex with her.

She liked me more than I liked her.

Scenario Two: I liked her more than she liked me.

I was raised in a lower-middle-class family, and I wasn't polished. Combine that with the fact that I was broke all the time and had a New York City attitude that said I'd rather punch you in the face than stab you in the back. I was rough around the edges.

I met a girl in college who I'll call Barb. Barb and I hit it off. There was chemistry. We hadn't crossed the line of sleeping together, but we didn't need to. We just meshed together and enjoyed being with each other. We'd been dating for a couple of weeks when her mom came to campus to check in on her.

Barb introduced me to her mom. She was nice, but I could feel her sizing me up. She visited for a day or two, and I respected their time together. When she left, I made my way to Barb's dorm and called her from a phone in the lobby. She came out of her room, but I sensed that something had changed.

"I can't see you anymore," Barb said.

I was shocked. "What are you talking about?"

"My mom doesn't approve of you, and she said I would regret being with you, and I needed to break it off before we got any closer."

"Are you kidding me? I really like you."

"I like you too," she said as she drew closer to me. Then she caught herself and pulled back.

"Barb, I don't want to not see you."

"My decision is final. I can't see you anymore."

As time passed, Barb made the Georgia Tech cheerleading team. Now I had to see her at every football game. Ugh! Then I saw her with her new man. He was polished, good-looking, and dressed in clothes I wouldn't be caught dead in. Preppy clothes with polished shoes, a button-down shirt, sometimes a tie, and maybe even a suit jacket. I wore the same pair of jeans every day for two weeks before I washed them.

Barb and I never spoke again. We didn't even wave to each other.

I liked her more than she liked me.

Scenario Three: We liked each other.

Sometimes I'd meet someone, and it would turn out that we liked each other equally. At the beginning of each year, the fraternities at Georgia Tech would have rush parties the first two weeks of school. At one of those parties, I saw her leaning against a railing on a rooftop deck. She looked at me, and for the first time, I noticed her beautiful blue eyes. Our eyes locked, and she smiled. Her smile was beautiful. I had to talk to her.

Fraternity parties were always packed with people. I had to work my way toward her. I could tell she knew I was coming. She blushed just enough for her cheeks to appear pink.

As I got close to her, she looked down. I paused long enough for her to look up at me.

"Hello," I said.

She looked at me with her beautiful eyes, and she couldn't stop smiling. "Hello."

"My name is Bruce. What's your name?"

"I'm Suzanne."

We talked the rest of the night. Suzanne was a native of Atlanta and lived in the suburbs. At the end of the night, I walked her to her car and said goodnight. We made plans to meet on campus the next day. I was a sophomore, and she was a freshman. We dated for five years.

We liked each other.

Recommendation:

Sometimes you'll meet people who you're attracted to, but you just don't match. Sometimes you don't like them as much as they like you. If they break up with you, you think, *Whew, I'm so glad that happened.*

When you happen to be on the short end of the deal, you like them more than they like you. When they break up with you, you need to mourn the loss and move on. I can remember the pain of someone I liked, or even loved, breaking up with me. I didn't handle it well. My method of handling it was to skip dinner and go straight to drinking for two to three weeks. That's not healthy, and it's not serving God.

Trust that God will put the right person in your life.

Get Married

Joy was the woman I started to date before my divorce was final. After the divorce, I continued to date Joy.

I told my therapist, "Joy is the one."

She looked me right in the eyes and said, "Under the circumstances, you know you were both married when your relationship started. The chances for this to work out are not good."

I didn't like that answer, and I replied, "Oh no, this is it."

My therapist was right. Joy broke up with me, and I was a mess. After about a month of serious mourning and drinking, I started to go out with my single buddies.

During one session, my therapist asked, "What do you want in a partner?"

I started to make a list of the qualities I was looking for. Within a few weeks, I had fifteen to twenty things scribbled all over the place. I sat down and tried to prioritize the list. I narrowed down the list to ten and put them in priority order. The first one was the most important, and the tenth one was important, but it was the least important of the ten. I also decided I wasn't going to sleep with anyone. I felt it was contrary to what Jesus wanted me to do, and I knew it clouded my thinking.

By this time, I was working in Miami. I'd go out with five or ten guys to clubs around town when I got this great idea.

I told my buddies, "I want you guys to pick the best-looking girl in here, and I'm going to walk up to her and say hello."

They all busted out laughing. One of them said, "Are you kidding?"

I said, "No, I'm not kidding."

We spent a few minutes discussing the women in the club and made a choice. I was just crazy enough to do it. About 50 percent of the time, I'd walk over to the girl, and she'd reject me before I got close. You know when a girl holds up her palm as if to say "stop" or waves her index finger as if to say, "don't even try it." Some would shake their heads and overexaggerate with their lips, saying, "No!" I'd turn around and head back to my friends, who would be in fits of laughter. After they calmed down, I'd have them choose someone else, and I'd walk over and say hello. Some of them were the nicest, friendliest people ever. I even got second and third dates with a few of them.

After these dates, I'd either go home and only be able to check off one of the top ten items on my list and never call the woman again, or they'd see my 1979 bottom-of-the-line Toyota Corolla when I came to pick them up, and they never called me again. There was one girl I dated a few times who I really liked. It got to the point where she came over to my condo and hinted she wanted to sleep with me. There was chemistry, but I wasn't going to cross that line. I walked her to her car and kissed her goodnight.

I worked with one of her girlfriends, and a couple of days later, that coworker came into my office and couldn't stop laughing.

"What's so funny?" I asked.

"That girl you went out with a few times asked me if you're gay."

"Wow! I knew she wanted to sleep with me. But I didn't want to cross that line."

"Trust me, I know. I told her you're not gay, but I don't think she believed me. She said she threw herself at you."

"She did, and I wanted her. But I made a commitment to myself that I'm not going to do that anymore."

We had a good laugh.

The corporate headquarters of Florida Power and Light in Miami was a large six-story building. The center of the building was hollow, with a large, open atrium. A glass roof covered the open area. The second through sixth floors had open-air walkways that ran around the interior of the building. In the atrium were a three-story-high waterfall and live foliage. Open-air escalators went from the first floor to the sixth floor, and you could walk off the escalator onto any floor.

One day, José Vazquez and I were riding the escalator. We were on the fourth floor, and I noticed a girl I'd liked for months down on the second floor.

I interrupted José and said, "I've been wanting to meet that girl for months."

In a matter-of-fact tone, José said, "That's Jan Friebertshauser, and she reports to me."

"Yeah, right. You are such an ass."

"No, I'm serious. She does."

"Yeah, sure."

We arrived on the fifth floor, where our offices were pretty close to each other. I was settling at my desk when José walked by my door—followed by Jan. He backed up a few steps and stuck his head in my door. Jan stopped in order not to crash into José and then backed up a few steps herself.

"Uh, hey, about that topic we were discussing," José said. "Can I pop back and catch up with you on that?"

I couldn't believe my eyes. "Sure. That would be great," I answered.

"Okay, good. Oh, have you ever met Jan? She's on my team."

I got up from behind my desk and walked to the door. "No, I haven't met Jan."

"Well, Jan is a CPA and an operational auditor. Jan, Bruce is one of the managers in the Management Services Team."

I shook her hand. "Hello, Jan. Nice to meet you."

Jan said, "Nice to meet you too."

I'd never seen her close up. I liked what I saw. And she was nice.

Five minutes later, José came bounding into my office, barely able to contain himself. In a low voice, I said, "You asshole, I am going to kick your ass."

"I told you she reported to me," José gloated.

I asked Jan out about five times over the next couple of months, but she always said no. I didn't know this, but she had been dating someone from Management Services in the Juno Beach office, about a ninety-minute drive north of Miami. They'd broken up, and she swore that she'd never date someone from work again.

The sixth time I asked her to go to lunch, she said, "Well, I'm really busy right now, and I don't think I am going to take lunch today."

That wasn't an unrealistic response for a CPA. But in my mind, that was it. I would never ask her out again.

Before I hit the hall, she jumped up and said, "If there's a group of people going to lunch, I'd be interested."

I was done. I said, "Okay," and headed back to my office. Five coworkers were waiting in my office. When I walked in, they knew I'd been rejected.

Someone piped up, "She said no again?"

Dejected, I said, "Yes, but this time with a stipulation. She said she'd go to lunch with a group."

The five of them jumped up and walked down the hall, poking their heads into every office. Eight people came back to my office and said, "We have a group going to lunch."

We all marched down to Jan's office, and I said, "A group from Management Services is going to lunch. Would you like to join us?"

"I would," she said.

We headed out, and Jan knew several of the people on the elevator. Small talk ensued. When the elevator stopped on the ground floor, Jan got out. I got out. But no one on the team got out.

One of them said, "Sorry, we forgot that we need to wrap a big project." Someone else pushed a button and the elevator doors closed.

I looked at Jan in shock. "I didn't know they were going to do that." I think she could tell that it was a surprise to me. "I'm sorry, do you want to go back to your office?" I asked.

"Well, we're here," she said. "Do you want to grab some lunch at the cafeteria?"

FPL had a great cafeteria in the building. "Yes, I would like to." It was a little awkward because the cafeteria was full, and we sat at a small table, just the two of us. We had a good conversation.

I walked her back to the elevator. When the doors opened, she could tell I wasn't getting on the elevator.

"Aren't you going back upstairs?" she asked.

"Not yet. I like to go across the street and get a Cuban coffee."

She looked at me. The elevator closed. "Do you mind if I go with you?" she asked.

"Of course not."

The people at the bodega knew me. I walked up and said, "Buenos días. Cómo estás? Dos Café Cubano, por favor."

Jan asked quietly, "Do you speak Spanish?"

"No, not really. I know a few words."

I found out later that I impressed her with my Spanish and with the way I treated the people at the bodega.

At the bodega, you stand outside and order through a window, where they serve the Café Cubano in little cups. A machine squeezes liquid sugar out of raw sugar canes that stick out of the top. A measured amount comes out into the coffee, and they stir it for you. The stainless-steel counter is large enough that several people can lean on it, chat, and enjoy the sunny Miami day. Jan and I talked as we sipped our coffee. She'd never had Café Cubano before, and she liked it. It gives you a nice kick after lunch.

Our first real date was July 4, 1989. She wouldn't go on a date with me unless it was with a group. I had a buddy from Georgia Tech who lived in Miami and planned to host a Fourth of July party for about twenty people. Jan would not let me pick her up. She drove herself.

We had a great time. When I got back home, I pulled out my list and checked the top nine boxes. I was stunned and thought, "*Holy Cow, Jan could be my wife someday.*"

To this day, I can't remember what number ten was. I can't remember all of the top nine either. But I do know that number one was that she had to believe in Jesus.

At some point, the not-having-sex issue came up. I told her I didn't want to before I got married and that I believed God didn't want me to either. We prayed about it, and Jan agreed with me. Somewhere around the ninth or tenth month, we broke that commitment, but on July 4, 1990—one year after our first date—I asked Jan to marry me in front of the house where she grew up in Wheeling, West Virginia. Her mom and dad were with us.

A few months later, Jan prepared to present an operations audit in front of a committee led by Jack Woodall, our manager's boss.

Before Jan started, Jack asked, "Jan, before you get into your presentation, I wanted to confirm something I heard. Is it true you're engaged to Bruce Sheridan?"

"Yes, I am."

Jack replied, "Well, your life will never be boring." Everyone in the room laughed.

We were married in March 1991 in North Palm Beach, Florida, by Pastor Lucky Arnold. My nerves were on edge as I stood at the altar. When Jan's father walked her down the aisle and Jan slipped her hand into mine, peace washed over me.

Recommendation:

Find the right person for you. Be diligent about the process. Having sex before marriage will cloud your judgment, and I don't recommend it. Find the right person and get married.

The second chapter of Genesis, the first book of the Bible, reads:

> So the man gave names to all livestock, the birds in the sky and all the wild animals.
>
> But for Adam no suitable helper was found. So the Lord God caused man to fall into a deep sleep; and while he was sleeping, he took one of the man's ribs and then closed up the place with flesh. Then the Lord God made a woman from the rib he had taken out of the man, and he brought her to the man.
>
> The man said, "This is now my bone of bones and flesh of my flesh; she shall be called 'woman,' for she was taken out of man."
>
> That is why a man leaves his father and mother and is united to his wife, and they become one flesh. Adam and his wife were both naked, and they felt no shame.
>
> Genesis 2:20-25

No one knows exactly when the book of Genesis was written. Scholars aren't even sure there was a written form at first. History in ancient culture was passed on in oral form. It's estimated Genesis was written down around 2,000 BC or roughly 4,000 years ago.

The New Testament books of the Bible were written later, roughly 2,000 years ago. Following are some New Testament verses on marriage:

> Some Pharisees came to him to test him. They asked, "Is it lawful for a man to divorce his wife for any and every reason?"
>
> "Haven't you read," he (Jesus) replied, "that at the beginning the Creator 'made them male and female,' and said, 'For this reason a man will leave his father and mother and be united to his wife, and the two will become one flesh.'" Therefore, what God has joined together, let no one separate.
>
> Matthew 19:3-6

> Submit to one another out of reverence for Christ. Wives, submit yourselves to your own husbands as you do to the Lord. For the husband is the head of the wife as Christ is the head of the church, his body, of which he is the Savior. Now as the church submits to Christ, so also wives should submit to their husbands in everything.
>
> Husbands, love your wives, just as Christ loved the church and gave himself up for her to make her holy, cleansing her by the washing with water through the word, and to present her to himself as a radiant church, without stain or wrinkle or any other blemish, but holy and blameless. In this same way, husbands ought to love their wives as their own bodies. He who loves his wife loves himself. After all, no one ever hated their own body, but they feed and care for their body, just as Christ does the church—for we are members of his body. "For this reason, a man will leave his father and mother and be united to his wife, and

the two will become one flesh." This is a profound mystery—but I am talking about Christ and the church. However, each one of you also must love his wife as he loves himself, and the wife must respect her husband.

Ephesians 5:21-33

13

GET STARTED

I often wonder why life seems to go faster as I get older. I remember being a young boy—in Sheridan Stage 1—waiting for the circus to come to Madison Square Garden in New York City. When my dad told me he got tickets, the circus would be three weeks away. Those three weeks felt like an eternity. Now, in 2022—in Sheridan Stage 7—three weeks sometimes feels like three minutes.

Over years of wrestling with this time issue, I developed a theory. When you're one year old, and you live another year and become two, that additional year equals a 100 percent increase in the time you've been alive. When you're 100 years old and live another year, that additional year increase equals a 1 percent increase in your lifespan. The differences in those percentages are dramatic.

Sheridan Stages of Life

Age	Stage	Percent of life	Traits
Birth to 8	1	100%	dependent
8 to 18	2	56%	puberty, physical growth, rebellion, independence
18–28	3	36%	rebellion, independence, love, marriage, feeling you're immortal, adulthood, divorce
28–38	4	26%	maturity, marriage, family, children
38–48	5	21%	prime years
48–58	6	17%	empty nester, grandchildren
58–68	7	15%	grandchildren, retirement
68–78	8	13%	memory loss, muscle loss, health issues
78–88	9	11%	frailty, loss of mobility, chronic illness
88+	10	10%	dependent

In the table above, I broke life into ten stages to show what percent of your life you live in each stage or decade. Assume you live to be sixty-eight. The last decade of your life represents 15 percent of your whole life. If you live to be ninety, the last decade of your life represents about 10 percent of your whole life. Two facts: one, we will all die, and two, you can only move to a higher Sheridan Stage. You can never go backward. Life moves on, and you need to take responsibility to live the best life you can.

Time nor tide waits for no one.

What Sheridan Stage are you in? My target audience is people in Stage 3, eighteen to twenty-eight years old. In 2022, I'm in stage 7. Why would a Sheridan Stage 3 listen to what a Sheridan Stage 7 has to say? First, you don't have to listen to me. Out of love and service to God, I want to share with you what I have learned by living through Stage 3 myself. I believe if Jesus had not come into my heart at age twenty-five, I might not have made it out of Stage 3 alive, or I could have landed in federal prison. Second, I want you to live a fulfilling and God-centered life throughout your entire life. Third, I've helped corporations for over thirty-five years create strategic plans and execute them. Companies that use strategic planning tools and techniques make these claims:

Time, nor tide, waits for no one.

- 73 percent say they improve revenue twice as fast.
- 73 percent say their profits are higher.
- 58 percent report they enjoy life more.
- 94 percent report they build better teams.

I want to combine the experience I've gained helping companies with my experience with Jesus to help you plan your life from this day forward. Let's get started.

How It All Started

Back in 1984, at Florida Power and Light Company (FPL), I was asked to help the Southern Division embrace the principles our CEO, Marshal McDonald, had observed on a trip to Japan.

Marshal visited Kansai Electric. While touring a customer service office, he saw a large board and asked what it was.

The interpreter informed him, "This is a Quality Storyboard. A meter reading team is improving their meter reading process. As you can see, they are below their target of twenty defects."

About the only thing Marshal understood on the chart was the numbers. Everything else was in Japanese. Marshal was feeling good. Our meter-reading team had a target of eight misread meters. Very few branches achieved the target, but most were close.

Marshall commented, "That's good performance, but at FPL, our teams mostly operate under ten defects per thousand."

The interpreter asked as politely as he could, "Mr. McDonald, did you say errors per thousand?"

"Yes."

"This team's target is to be below twenty misread meters per million."

Per million! Marshal thought. *If we are eight per thousand, that means 8,000 per million. We have 4.4 million customers. That's over 35,000 misread meters per month. If they are at twenty misread meters per million, they would have less than ninety misread meters per month.*

Marshal was in such disbelief that he asked them to get another interpreter to verify what he'd just heard. It was true. The Kansai Electric meter reading teams were below twenty misread meters per million.

When he returned to Miami, he insisted that we figure out how Kansai Electric ran their company. We discovered that they were following the Deming Prize for Quality methodology. My new role was to figure out how we could adopt that same methodology. The Miami Division was so big that FPL split the Division into East and West. Two of us were assigned, one to each VP, to get the ball rolling.

Over the next five years, we took FPL from a below-average electric utility to one of the best in the nation, using the Deming Prize methodology. The Deming Prize methodology started with creating a well-informed strategic plan that included a process for rolling it out throughout the entire company. It took years to get it right.

I've spent my career helping companies create their strategy and execute against that strategy. I never imagined I'd use these skills to help young people create a strategy for their life. But I did, and I continue to do so.

My oldest son, Andrew, graduated from college in 2015. He got a bachelor's in sports management from North Carolina State University. Everywhere he looked for a job, they said he could work for free to start. Remember, I'd gotten Andrew a summer internship in 2011 with Barclays Bank in London in the Anti-Money Laundering Department, and in the summer of 2012, an internship at Madison Square Garden in New York City in the chief of revenue's department. Even with that wealth of experience and a four-year degree, he still couldn't land a job. He took a sales position at LifeTime Fitness.

"Dad, I don't like sales," he said. "I want to do something else."

I said, "Great, what do you want to do?"

His reply? "I don't know."

I felt frustrated. I love my children, and when they hurt, I hurt. For several months, he continued to say he wasn't happy. When I'd ask him what he wanted to do, he would repeat, "I don't know." It hit me that for thirty-five years, I'd been helping large and small businesses figure out their strategy and put together a plan for them to execute against their strategy. If I could do that for a company, why couldn't I do that for my son?

I asked, "Would you be willing to sit down with me to see if we can figure out your job situation, decide what you want to do, and create a plan?"

"Sure, Dad. I can do that."

One Saturday afternoon, I grabbed a pen and a few sheets of blank paper, and we sat down at the kitchen table.

I started by asking him, "What do you want to do?"

Andrew again said, "I don't know."

I was squirming inside. For months, Andrew had said he didn't know what he wanted to do. I wracked my brain, wondering how to guide him. I felt stumped but then had a moment of clarity.

"I want you to imagine that there are no constraints. Nothing holding you back. You can do whatever you want. Imagine you jump out of bed in the morning and can't wait to get to work. Remember, no constraints. Don't worry about money, education—nothing can hold you back. What would that job be?" I asked.

Andrew answered, "I don't know."

If someone had asked me that question at his age, I would have said I wanted to be a fighter pilot, a gold medal Olympian in the high hurdles, a pediatrician, a pastry chef in Manhattan, an FBI Agent—and that's just off the top of my head. I was shocked by his answer.

I looked him in the eyes and said, "I want you to do one thing for me. Can you promise to do one thing for me.?"

"Uh, yeah, what is it?"

"I want you to promise me you will try really hard not to blurt out 'I don't know' when I ask you a question."

"Okay, I'll try."

"Take as long as you need to answer, but don't say 'I don't know.' When you say that, it immediately stops you from thinking. Now, I'm going to ask my question again.

"If you could have any job in the world, what would it be?"

I could see him struggle not to say, "I don't know." His mind was working overtime.

After a few moments, he said with a big smile on his face, "I'd be a pro-sports agent."

"Yes!" I shouted.

We decided that he should look for a job with a sports organization. He also needed to research what it would take to apply to law school. To be an agent for professional athletes, he'd need a law degree. We spent nearly four hours writing out a strategy. We focused on his relationship with God, his relationship with friends and family, and his career, and we made the first draft of his budget. The hours felt like fifteen minutes.

"Dad, this was awesome. I know a lot of my friends could use this type of coaching. It has helped me so much, and I know it would help them," Andrew said.

A year later, I started Life Compass, a 501c3 nonprofit. Life Compass's positioning statement has not changed. "We serve God by coaching young adults to plan and live a fulfilling, God-centered life because God loves them completely."

Create Your Plan

Research has shown that people who think about their future, write down goals, track their progress, and review their overall plan at least every three months will make greater progress than someone who takes life one day at a time without a plan. I can attest from working for over thirty-five years with more than two hundred business owners that it works in the business world.

Here is Life Compass's Four-Step Proven Process that you can get started on today. Ideally, schedule a time to talk to a Life Compass Coach. If you are hesitant, work on your own or with a trusted pastor, minister, priest, therapist, counselor, coach, or parent. The key is to get started.

- **Step 1**: Take time to think about where you want to go with your life. Try not to put any limits on yourself, like "I'm not smart enough," "I don't have enough money to do this," "I have no experience," and so forth. Lock out the negative and dream big dreams.
- **Step 2:** Write down your dreams. At first, you may want to change them every week. This takes time. Sheridan Stage 3, eighteen to twenty-eight years old, is the best time to try new things. If you want to shift your dreams, do it.
- **Step 3:** Monitor your progress. This is a way to hold yourself accountable. If you're not checking your progress on a regular basis, days turn into weeks, weeks turn into months, and months turn into years. Before you know it, the years have passed, and you've made little to no progress on your dreams.
- **Step 4:** Review your plan. Review your plan and update it whenever you want to make a change. Studies have shown people lose focus at about the ninety-day mark. Review your plan at least once every three months.

Let's dig a little deeper into each step.

Step 1: Think

Take quiet time to sit alone with no distractions, no TV, smartphone, computer, tablet, or other electronic devices. Use a pad of paper and capture your thoughts about the following:

a. Question: "Imagine it's three years from today. Looking back on your life, both personally and professionally, what needs to happen for you to consider your life successful?"
b. Make sure you cover these five categories.
   - God
   - Friends and Family
   - Career
   - Budget
   - Risks
c. Think about and write down what you need to focus on over the next six to twelve months in each category. Prioritize and select the top one to five goals in each area. Selecting more than five goals is too much.
d. Ask your parents, trusted friends, pastors, and mentors for input on what you have created so far.

Step 2: Write

Write down your goals using the S.M.A.R.T. approach. Goals should be:

a. **Specific**—be as specific as possible. Can someone decisively tell if you accomplished the goal?

- Bad Example: Do a better job in school.
  Good Example: Get at least a B in all my classes.
- Bad Example: Lose weight.
  Good Example: Lose ten pounds over the next three months.

b. **Measurable**—Quantitative is best. Qualitative is okay.
   - Quantitative Example: Lose ten pounds in the next six months.
   - Qualitative Example: Look better in six months.

You can *measure* how many pounds you lost, and if you lost ten or more, you hit the goal. How you look is someone's opinion, and it can be different for every person. It is a lot harder to tell if you hit the goal "look better."

c. **Attainable**—Don't set your goal so high that it isn't attainable. Set a stretch goal, but not an impossible goal. If you set impossible goals, you won't hit them, and you'll get frustrated.
   - Impossible Goal: Climb Mount Everest in thirty days.
   - Attainable Goal: Walk two miles three times per week.

d. **Relevant**—Select goals that are important to you and relevant to your life and your dreams.

e. **Time-bound**—Set a due date. Try to keep it to what you can accomplish in three to six months. Try to keep those deadlines within the next twelve months. Setting goals any further out than a year may promote procrastination.

Enter your goals into the Life Compass app (Apple store: "Life Comp" or Android: "Life Compass") or keep track on a spreadsheet or even on a sheet of paper.

Step 3: Track

If you're using the Life Compass App, you will track your progress daily. Each day, you can enter green, yellow, or red against your progress for each goal.

> ***Green***: You feel you're right on track or even ahead of where you expected to be. You're happy with your progress and feel good about achieving your goal.
>
> ***Yellow***: You fell short of your expectations. You made progress, but you know you could be doing better.
>
> ***Red***: You did little or nothing to make progress against your goal.

Keep track of your progress over time. The Life Compass app will provide a seven-day, thirty-day, and since-the-beginning-of-the-goal graphic to track progress. The objective is to see progress toward 100 percent green.

Step 4: Review

One thing that is constant in life is change. Maslow's Hierarchy of Needs has five levels. They are:

1. Survival. Will I live until the end of the day? People all over the world struggle with this question on a daily basis.
2. Security. Do I have shelter or a home? Am I safe? Again, millions of people in the world and in the US cannot answer yes to this question.
3. Community. Do I belong to a group? Am I surrounded by people I like and trust?

4. Ego. Can I be a leader in my community?
5. Self-Actualization. When you reach this stage, you feel complete and secure in your life. You are doing what you want to do.

Your life can be tossed between any of the five levels at a moment's notice. For example, if you were in the World Trade Center on September eleventh, or your doctor just told you that you have a fatal disease, or you learn you're being evicted from your home. You're back to level one or two. Many changes in our lives are not as dramatic; however, things do change, and you'll need to adjust your Life Compass.

Review your entire set of goals at least once every three months. Your Life Compass is here to support you throughout this journey. For more information, go to the website lifecomp.org.

14

FINAL WORDS

All this I have spoken while still with you. But the Advocate, the Holy Spirit, whom the father will send in my name, will teach you all things and will remind you of everything I have said to you. Peace I leave you; my peace I give to you. I do not give to you as the world gives. Do not let your hearts be troubled and do not be afraid.

John 14:25-27

"The first hundred years are brutal."
– Frank Sheridan (1930–2018)

All day long, there's a voice inside my head. The Voice makes decisions. While I'm trying to make a decision, the Voice may hold a debate. The speed at which the Voice makes decisions is astounding. How do I know if the Voice is making the right decision? Am I in charge of the Voice? I'm not sure.

In the United States, we have laws to help the Voice make legally correct decisions. Most people I know have gotten a speeding ticket. When I was in high school, my cousin was shot through the heart. Even the threat of breaking the law and the possibility of going to prison cannot always silence the Voice.

Why do we listen to the Voice when it's telling us to do something that's going to hurt us or someone else? I believe it's because there's good and evil in this world. I try to start every day with a prayer like this:

"LORD Almighty, maker of heaven and earth, you are the Holy One; you are the Lord Most High. God the Father, God the Son, and God the Holy Spirit, use me today to fulfill your will. I pray that the Living God, the Holy Spirit, fills me up to overflowing and protects me from the evil one. *(Sometimes I can feel the Holy Spirit come into my body. I feel muscles relax that I didn't realize were tense, I feel my heartbeat slow down, and I feel an overwhelming love and peace wash over me.)* God, I lay everything I have at your feet. My mind, my heart, every cell in my body, my time, and all my resources are yours, God. Direct me, LORD, in the way I should go. Help me to love everyone who crosses my path and to forgive those who trespass against me."

Often when I pray that prayer, right in the middle of it, the Voice interrupts and sends my mind off in a different direction. Sometimes it's a sinful thought. I catch myself and get angry and think, *What are you doing? I'm praying here.* If it was a sinful thought, I pray for forgiveness and return to my original prayer. Occasionally, I don't make it back to my original prayer.

At the time I'm writing this, I'm in Sheridan Stage 7. For over sixty years, I've been battling the Voice in my head to keep it in check and stop it from hurting myself and others. I've chosen the Bible, the Word of God, as my source for deciding right from wrong. I read the Word almost every day. Sometimes the Voice still convinces me to go against the Word of God. I call that sin. If I were put on a desert island, I know the Voice would still cause me to sin. Inside us all, there's a battle between good and evil.

I've chosen the Bible, the Word of God, as my source for deciding right from wrong. I read the Word almost every day.

Please stop for one moment, clear everything in your head, quiet the Voice, and listen to what I am about to say. You are wonderfully made. YOU ARE WONDERFULLY MADE.

You deserve to be loved and live a good life. Jesus Christ loves you. God the Father loves you. The Holy Spirit loves you. I love you. But one of the most difficult things to do in life is to love yourself. If you can manage that, then with God's help, you can meet any goal you can imagine.

I am begging you, cajoling you, and pleading with you to take control of your life as best you can. Manage the Voice inside your head as best you can. Make better choices. Let Jesus come into your heart and into your life. Let the Holy Spirit work with you and in you. Spend the rest of your life knowing that no matter what comes your way, God can get you through it. Through Jesus, you will receive the promise of eternal life with God in heaven. Imagine no darkness, like going down into the basement at night. No lies, like when someone you loved and trusted hurt you deeply. No hate, like the bully who trashed you on social media. Heaven will be love, light, and truth.

I wish you the best as you journey through your life. It's not easy. You'll stumble. Bad things will happen to you. The ones you love will stumble. Bad things will happen to them. Invite

Jesus into your heart, invite the Living God here on Earth, the Holy Spirit, to live in your heart and to walk with you all the days of your life. I believe the best chance you have to live an intentional life is with God in your heart. May God bless you.

ABOUT THE AUTHOR

Bruce Sheridan embraces mystery. Raised in Union City, New Jersey, the fourth child in a family of eight, his life was never boring. Union City is the home of the entrance to the Lincoln Tunnel, which connects New Jersey to New York City. It's a tough town. The author estimates he had participated in six hundred fights by the time he graduated from high school.

In 1977, Bruce headed off to Georgia Tech to study engineering. He was on the Men's Varsity track team and ran the 110M high hurdles and the 400M intermediate hurdles. In 1988, he was a member of the US Virgin Islands Olympic Sailing Team.

With degree in hand, he headed to Miami, Florida, in 1981. As an engineer for Florida Power and Light, he designed and built the power grid that supplies electricity to residential and commercial enterprises. Attending graduate school at night, he earned his Master of Science in Industrial Engineering from the University of Miami. He also earned his Professional Engineering License from the State of Florida.

Bruce has worked for large corporations like General Electric and Bank of America. For many years, he's been an entrepreneur running his own coaching business and helping entrepreneurs. Bruce implements the Entrepreneurial Operating System, EOS®.

In 1984, Bruce fell on his knees and asked God to save his life. God answered that prayer. Ever since then, he's been a warrior for God.

In 1993, the American Society for Quality published Bruce's first book, *Policy Deployment: The Total Quality Management Approach to Long-Range Planning.*

Bruce has been married to Jan since 1991, and they have four awesome sons, a daughter-in-law, a granddaughter, an Irish Wheaten Terrier, and a tabby cat. He enjoys riding his Harley-Davidson motorcycle, golfing, camping, time at the beach, and serving at his church.

ABOUT LIFE COMPASS

Life Compass Incorporated began 2015, as a 501c3 non-profit ministry to help young adults create a course for their future. A compass points true north, and the goal of Life Compass is to help you create a true north for your life. Unlike with a traditional compass, you can change course and reset your own true north if it isn't leading you where you want to go.

Life Compass has three offerings. The first is this book. We hope that you'll find value in the lessons presented here. All proceeds from the sale of this book go back into the Life Compass ministry. Our second offering is one-on-one coaching, a free-of-charge service to give you a more focused experience. Our third offering is an app you can use to track your progress as you go about creating your life. The Life Compass app is free and can be downloaded on our website, www.lifecomp.org. You can also download the app by using your smart phone camera now. Here's how:

Open the camera on your phone. Point the camera at the appropriate QR Code below for the type of phone you have. Follow the directions on the screen after the QR Code is read.

For Apple iPhone:

For Android phone:

CPSIA information can be obtained
at www.ICGtesting.com
Printed in the USA
JSHW031929190522
26003JS00001B/8